# Peter Urs Bender

# SECRETS OF

# P·O·W·E·R

# PRESENTATIONS

**Focusing on Effective, Dynamic and
Impressive Business**

D0905583

## FIREFLY BOOKS

# A FIREFLY BOOK

**Cataloguing in Publication Data**

Bender, Peter Urs., 1944-
  Secrets of power presentations

Rev. ed.
ISBN 1-895565-57-X

1. Public speaking.  2. Business communication.
3. Self-presentation.  4. Success in business.
I. Title.

HF5718.22.B45 1995   658.4'52   C95-930396-0

---

Published by:

Firefly Books Inc.
250 Sparks Avenue
Willowdale, ON  M2H 2S4

Firefly Books (U.S.) Inc.
P.O. Box 1325
Ellicott Stn.,
Buffalo, NY  14205

Typesetting and Design by:
Final Edition Graphics Inc.

Cover Design by:
Sheila McGraw

Printed and bound in Canada

# Preface

If two equally educated and qualified people offer similar solutions to a problem . . . undoubtedly – the one who knows how to present with power – will always have a much better chance of having their ideas implemented.

This book does not need to be read from beginning to end. You can use it like a reference manual – each chapter, part and subtitle is designed as a stand alone module.

However, for optimum results – you should read it at least three times from cover to cover. Use a pen or pencil to circle and underline the ideas which you think can help for your next presentation.

Also, share the new-found techniques in this book with a co-worker or a friend. It is easier to get feedback from a person who knows the secrets which make great presentations.

Good luck and all the best in the continuous improvement of your presentation skills.

To all those
with
**DYSLEXIA**

# Mission Statement

**This book will give you a full awareness
of a Power Presentation
in a business environment
with improved results for both
you and your company.**

*You can either take action,
or you can hang back
and hope for a miracle.
Miracles are great,
but they are
so unpredictable.*

*-Peter F. Drucker*

# Acknowledgements

This book is the culmination of many years experience as a speaker in the business world. The ideas I will share with you are not new, but they are assembled together for the first time in one convenient guide.

My knowledge has been gained from presentations made over the years, from listening to friends, reading books, and making mistakes.

Several others helped me develop these ideas: my colleagues in business, peers at the National Speakers Association, clients, and my former students.

I have tested each idea quite a few times before real audiences, and so you can rest assured, they really do work!

Having dyslexia, a learning disability, and suffering through school did not help much in writing my book. However, I had a lot of input from others.

In particular, I wish to thank Michael McClintock for helping to develop and edit the manuscript based on my ideas. Mike graduated with an M.A. in Political Science from the University of Toronto. He then attended two of my courses, at Ryerson University: Effective Persuasion and Public Speaking. In both, he obtained an A+, which only a very few students ever achieve. Mike also worked with me for some time as an assistant. He had the opportunity to observe many of my presentations to various audiences. He has directed me to communicate the essential points in as few words as possible. Mike himself is now a pro in presenting and some of the concepts I will share with you actually came from him. I wish Mike the very best as he advances in his challenging and rewarding business career.

As well, I thank Jill Scott of Greenfield Projects for her talent in creating the drawings in the book.

Many thanks to Dr. Martin Kates and Martin Ossip who also read the manuscript and made helpful comments and suggestions. The book is a better one because of their contributions.

Last but not least, I thank my wife, Francie, who took the time to edit my work and give it a more polished look. Without her thoughtful input it would not be what it is.

# Powerful, Impressive and Lasting Presentations Start from Within:

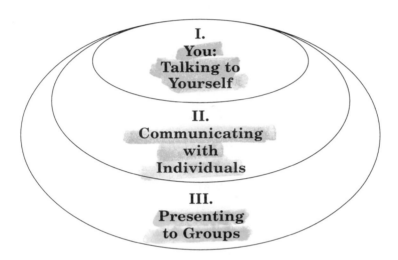

I.    You must talk to yourself. Clarify the message in your own mind before you communicate it to your audience.

II.    When you speak to individuals, express your thoughts in an organized manner. Clarify. Ask for feedback. Do not assume that the message sent is the message received.

III.    When presenting to a group, use the ideas discussed in this book. Your chances of being understood and accepted will increase dramatically.

# TABLE OF CONTENTS

*The people who get on
in this world
are the people who
get up and look for the
circumstances they want,
and if they can't find them,
make them.*

*- George Bernard Shaw*

# STEPS TO BETTER COMMUNICATION

## Why Are Presentations Skills So Important Today?

**M**uch is being said these days about the keys to advancement in the world of business. What is the fundamental determinant to your future success? Knowledge, technical skills, experience and organizational ability are all important to your career advancement.

Communication, however, is critical. How well you communicate with your staff, peers, managers, and for that matter, any group that you address is the key to advancement in your career.

## What Is Effective Communication?

Communication refers to the conveying of ideas to other people. Effective communication takes place when you share your message with others in such a manner that it is clearly understood. People who communicate effectively are able to:

- Exercise leadership
- Inspire staff and colleagues to take action
- Obtain trust and respect
- Have more fun with people
- Get others to feel more confident about themselves
- Convey information easily and accurately
- Achieve their goals
- Reach their objectives

# The World of Communication

If two otherwise equally qualified individuals compete for the same senior position in an organization, most of the time the one with better communications skills gets the job. Information and the ability to convey it is power.

But it is not just speech. Communication takes place in many forms - audio, visual, sensual - through sounds, images, and physical impulses. It consists of talking, listening, looking, touching, tasting, feeling, smelling, acting and much more.

It can involve sending messages through photographs, posters, books, newspapers, magazines, television, radio, recorded sound, video tape, computers, fax machines, and other forms of electronic telecommunication.

Everything you do and everything around you communicates messages. There are unlimited ways for you to organize ideas and communicate them to others.

Today we are experiencing an information and communications explosion. Years ago it seemed possible to give full attention to just about all the important ideas we heard in any given day. There were only a few television stations to choose from and only a handful of monthly news publications, popular magazines and newly published books in any given week.

Today, our choices are unlimited. There are more books and magazines to read, movies and television programs to watch, and speeches and lectures to listen to than we can possibly digest in a single lifetime.

Look in any bookstore, library, video outlet, or at the number of different courses available in any university. We are so swamped with "communications opportunities" that we cannot absorb all of the messages being conveyed.

There is so much communication going on in our world that it is very difficult to decide what we should pay attention to. We must make such choices quickly to keep up with the flow of data to which we are exposed. To cope, we tend to give our attention first to those ideas which "grab" us most like the ones that are creatively conveyed to hold our interest.

Because of today's information explosion we must learn to compete with all of the other messages out there. It is critical that we communicate as quickly and effectively as we can.

The challenge in today's world is to capture other people's attention – to get them to turn their concentration away from others and focus on us and our ideas.

## Master the Tools of Communication

Successful communication demands that you take advantage of all the modern skills and aids available to ensure that your message comes across as you intend it. The conveying of ideas takes place in several dimensions at once.

> *I hear - I forget.*
> *I see - I remember.*
> *I do - I understand*
> — *Confucius*

It takes more than just words to communicate an experience to others. You must involve your listeners in what you are saying. They must experience your message using all of their senses: sound, sight and touch - even smell and taste.

# What This Book Is Not About

I will not be talking about traditional public speaking skills in this book. In the past, texts and courses on public speaking focused narrowly on the art of speech - that is, the words you use to get your ideas across. I define "speech" in a very specific way. Indeed, the content of *what* you say is important. You must have a message to share with other people before you can communicate. However, I focus on *how* you communicate. Successful presentations involve speech, but also involve an entire approach using many tools, which I will call, the "Presentation". This is the overall process by which you bring your message across as effectively and accurately as possible, using different techniques and communication aids. The "speech" is only part of the process.

# How is this Book Different from Others on Communication?

Other books tell you how to choose your topic, how to organize what you will say and that's about all. Because there is so much to making a presentation besides the content of your speech, I have emphasized all of those critical things which public speaking books leave out. We will look at such topics as how to use body language to the fullest, how to rehearse, how to use visual aids, how to use external equipment, and how to prepare literally every detail to ensure a smooth and perfect presentation!

Other public speaking handbooks emphasize the theory of communication and provide general ideas as to how to relate your topic to the audience. This book tells you all of the practical secrets you need to master when delivering your message.

# What You Heard is Not What I Meant...

Too often, we assume that because we are trying so hard to communicate, everyone will automatically understand us. Nothing could be more untrue!

This reminds me of the story of the tourist travelling in a foreign country. Not knowing the language, he yells loudly at the natives thinking that he will be better understood! They, of course, think he is nuts.

Most of the time, people simply do not say what they mean. We often confuse others by not conveying things in simple, familiar terms. Listeners judge you by what *they* think you said, rather than what was intended. It does not matter that your intention was not to hurt the other's feelings, if what you said did indeed hurt.

The meaning of your message is determined by the reaction you get from other people. Your intentions are not important if others do not understand you.

A wise man once observed:

**"I know that you believe you understand what you think I said, but, I am not sure you realize that what you heard is not what I meant...."**

I always thought that sounded funny, smart and witty—until I started to write this book . . . . Now I understand what it means!

Do you emphasize understanding when you communicate, as opposed to agreement?

Do you put in every effort to make it easy for others to understand you?

Here are some common mistakes people make when trying to communicate. These apply to speaking to a group as well as to an individual:

## Traps to Avoid In Public Speaking

- Talking too rapidly
- Speaking in a monotone
- Using too high a vocal pitch
- Not smiling enough while talking
- Talking and not saying much
- Presenting without enough emotion or passion
- Using too many "big" words
- Using abstractions without giving concrete examples
- Not explaining the meaning of words and expressions
- Using unfamiliar technical jargon
- Not introducing the message and its relevance clearly
- Using poor grammar
- Talking so quietly that people cannot hear
- Using slang or profanity
- Talking without preparation or knowledge of the topic
- Disorganized and rambling performance
- Not making proper eye contact with listeners
- Fidgety behavior that distracts the listeners
- Talking down to the audience
- Indirect communication i.e. beating around the bush
- Not summarizing and concluding the message clearly
- Failing to use visual aids to illustrate points
- Insulting the audience's intelligence
- Not asking for action

Do you do any of these things? Everyone is sure to be guilty of at least one, but recognition is the key to improvement! Just looking at this list of traps, it is easy to see how the message is not all that is important when communicating verbally.

What good is it if no one can understand or even hear you? What good is it if your style alienates the audience?

The purpose of your presentation should be, foremost, to be heard, and second, to be understood. Having done this, if things are going well, you can work on getting the listeners to agree with you and take the action you want.

## Five Sure Ways to Kill a Presentation

- **Do not make eye contact with your audience**

- **Make people feel stupid - Talk down to them**

- **Tell them just the facts - Nothing but the facts**

- **Do not get excited - Keep it boring - Do not use any body language**

- **Do not smile at all**

# THE PROCESS OF COMMUNICATING

There is a series of six steps we all go through to enable others to understand us. Simply put, communication is the process of sending and receiving messages. But it is not complete until feedback is obtained from the listener.

## 1. Have a Message Worth Communicating

You must have a worthwhile message and you must be *ready* to communicate it. We have all met people who do not know what they are talking about and yet they persist in babbling away. The saying goes, "Don't put your mouth in motion before your mind is in gear". It takes time and practice to organize your thoughts before you speak. However, time in preparation is a very important investment when you consider the high payoff you can receive.

## 2. Gain the Listeners' Attention, Capture their Interest, Build their Trust

Everyone asks, "What's in it for me?" Plain statements, without regard to the needs and desires of people, beg the response, "So what?". Unless you relate your message to something of interest to the listeners, you will not maintain their attention for very long. You must obtain their trust in order to persuade them to your way of thinking. If the audience does not have confidence in you, they will not believe what you say. Establish trust at the beginning of your presentation, not at the end. The ancient Greeks knew that "no one is interested in you until you are interested in them!" Show that you are trying to give your audience something they want.

# 3. Emphasize Understanding

Focus foremost on making yourself *understood*. Do not try to persuade and do not worry about proving that you are right (Not yet, anyway). Be careful of your tone of voice and do not lecture or condescend! No mature adult likes to be talked to this way.

# 4. Obtain Feedback

Test to see if your presentation is taking your audience down the right path. Find out if they understand you. If they do not, stop and clarify what you mean. Try again and again if necessary to illustrate your point.

Be patient with your listeners. See things from their point of view. It is *not their fault* if they do not understand you. It just means that you did not communicate clearly.

# 5. Watch Your Emotional Tone

Here is one of the most peculiar conversational phenomena: Have you ever noticed that two people may sound as if they disagree even when they are saying the same thing? Some individuals just like to argue. They do not really listen or recognize when they are on the same side of an issue. Do not allow argumentative tones and strong emotions to interfere with your message.

When communicating with people, whose emotions are aroused, acknowledge as early as possible that you understand and agree with what they are saying. Doing this will help calm them so that your message can be heard.

# 6. Persuade Them

This is the last step and perhaps the most important one for you. Once you are confident that your listeners have understood you, then and only *then*, focus on *persuading* them to adopt your point of view and take the action you want.
Always remember:

### *We only do things to gain a benefit or to avoid a loss!*

Be sure you tell your audience *why* they should take the action you ask them to. Persuasion will be much easier *after* you have deliberately gone through the first five steps.

### Your audience must understand your message before they can agree with you !

Your success in getting people to agree with you depends on your mastery of *all* the tools of communication available to you, not just the content of your speech. Getting your audience to understand you is what this book is all about.

# THE SPEECH VERSUS THE PRESENTATION

The speech is your message in its most basic form. It contains your ideas and the words you use to express them. However, the presentation conveys your message in multi-media form, utilizing your voice, body language, visual aids and various other techniques to involve your audience. It is the total image you convey to your audience. Just as a chain is only as strong as its weakest link, your presentation requires preparation and skilled delivery.

My approach has five components, what I call:

## The Five Essential Elements of a Power Presentation

  I.  The Speech
  II.  Body Language
  III. Equipment
  IV. The Environment
  V.  Preparation

# THE FIVE ESSENTIAL PARTS OF A POWER PRESENTATION

Attention to each of these components is essential if you want to have an impact on your audience. Let's take a quick look at each part:

**I. The Speech** - In this section I will tell you how to refine your ideas and the words you use to express them. In your speech you can either inform, entertain, touch the audience emotionally, or move them to action. *But*, you *must* do one of these four things or your effort is not a real "speech". If you have no such objective you are wasting time - yours and your audiences. Therefore, it is very important that you know why you are speaking and what you are trying to accomplish with your listeners.

**II. Body Language** - Here, we will discuss the use of your body's physical communication tools: voice, breathing, facial expressions, eye contact, gestures, posture, movement, physical energy, and how you are dressed.

**III. Use of Equipment** - This important section will review how you can make use of the presentation aids available today: handouts, models, drawings, pictures, charts, overheads, flipcharts, whiteboards, films, videos, slides, recordings, and microphones.

**IV. The Environment** - Here I will give you tips on *where* and *when* to present, including: location and size of the room, temperature, layout and seating, the speaking platform, entrances and exits, refreshments, background music, lighting, breaks, restrooms, and the timing of your presentation.

**V. Preparation** - The most critical element of any presentation is the preparation and rehearsal of literally every detail in advance. In this section, I will review how to prepare your speech, body language, and handouts as well as cover such important points as knowing your audience, knowing how to open and close, and ensuring that your presentation is properly introduced. I will explain the importance of confirming your presentation date, time and place, setting up the room and equipment, and testing the microphones. I will also discuss working with meeting organizers.

Understanding and applying these five essential elements of a power presentation clearly makes the difference in how well you impact on audiences.

Too many people focus on only the first part, the speech, and then wonder why they have no impact! However, communication using all the senses of sound, sight, and physical touch guarantees that your message will be better understood.

Skillful incorporation of these five components of a presentation will ensure that no one misses your point – whether they agree with you or not. If they do not, at least you will have done everything possible to convey your message in the most powerful way!

## What is the Number One Fear of Adults Living in the Western World?

Strange as it may seem, what many human beings fear more than death is public speaking! Most people believe that talking in front of a group provides one of the greatest opportunities for humiliation. Most of us are afraid of saying the wrong thing and making fools of ourselves. However, we all admire those who can confidently get up in front of large gatherings and talk without notes, as though the situation were a one-to-one conversation. The fact is, we are *all* capable of developing better skills at public speaking. We can *all* be more confident and effective in communicating our ideas to a group. It takes time, training, and practice, but we can get better at it. To make better presentations we must be willing to risk failure.

We all experience situations where we aren't sure what to say. It's embarrassing to be speechless. The stress of the position we are in often makes it hard to concentrate. Sometimes we try so hard to remember everything we want to cover that we end up forgetting everything.

There are times when we feel we really do not know what we are talking about, yet others demand that we give our opinion anyway! Other times we try so hard to make a favorable impression that we are unable to relax and be ourselves.

Have you ever had a "brownout", a situation where suddenly you forgot what you were thinking and didn't know what to say?

Brownouts are natural and can be handled smoothly. The secret to preventing them is to prepare note cards. (For more details see page 68. If you really do not know what to say, shut up until you do. If you do not know the answer to a difficult audience question, or you forget an important detail while speaking, simply say so and pledge sincerely to find out the answer later.

## Worst Human Fears

1. Speaking in front of a group
2. Dying
3. Speaking and dying in front of a group

# Desire and Persistence: The Keys to Success

Everyone who has ever accomplished an outstanding task knows that it takes many failures to gain one success. Most achievers do not make it on the first try. However, they believe so much in what they are doing that they simply cannot quit. They have the guts to keep going and the ability to analyse their mistakes to determine where they need to improve.

This is how athletes win Olympic gold medals, scientists make great discoveries and entrepreneurs launch successful new businesses. It is also how you will become a powerful, master presenter.

1. *You* must *want* to be a better presenter!
2. *You* must *believe* in yourself 100% in order for your efforts to pay off.

Become passionate about your message and your ability to communicate it. Pursue the goal of excellence in both knowledge of your topic and your ability to present it. Half-hearted wishing will only bring disappointing results.

If you do not sincerely desire to develop your skills, you will give up too soon and your efforts will have been wasted!

Persistence and self-improvement go hand in hand. After all, you cannot improve unless you try and you cannot improve if you give up too soon. But most of all, you cannot improve if you do not know what you want to accomplish!

As the saying goes, "If you don't know where you are going, any road will get you there." Therefore, once you know the areas in need of improvement, you will know where you should focus your attention and energy.

Some people may need to develop more confidence in speaking to a group. Others may need to create a more interesting style. Some should polish their skills in one or two areas to give them the extra edge. In each case the secrets are the same:

  – Analyse your weak points and then improve!

  – Know your strengths and build on them.

  – Develop a plan of action for improving your technique. Then, keep practicing until you get it perfectly right! It might take you one attempt or it might take one hundred. It might happen the first time or it might take a year. However, you must persist or you will not make any progress at all!

---

### *Persistence*

*Nothing in the world can take the place of persistence.*
*Talent will not: Nothing is more common than unsuccessful people with talent.*
*Genius will not: Unrewarded genius is almost a proverb.*
*Education will not: the world is full of educated derelicts.*
*Persistence and determination alone are omnipotent.*

*— Calvin Coolidge*

---

I want to be honestly open and brutally frank with you. Nothing great will happen without effort, sweat, tears and lots of preparation. . .

It doesn't matter if you have an M.B.A., a PhD or a high school diploma. If you are a President or have a million in a Swiss bank account you must still learn the hard way to make powerful and impressive presentations. To paraphrase Thomas Edison, learning to present effectively takes 10% inspiration and 90% perspiration!

## Study Other Presenters

The best and simplest way to improve is to pay attention to other presenters and analyse what they do. Observe the great ones and also the beginners. Determine what it is that makes the good ones good and the bad ones bad.

Do this every time you hear a speech or see a presentation. Then examine your own style and make adjustments.

Persist. Do not expect immediate results. It takes time to become a master. But *you* have it *in you* to become one.

## Appraise Your Presentation Skills

Refer to the checklist in the Appendix, entitled "How to Evaluate Yourself". Go through the exercise thinking of the last time you made a presentation - it doesn't matter whether you were talking to just a few people or fifty!

Did you prepare your message well in advance? Did you have a clearly defined objective? Did you rehearse all or part of what you said? Did you have rapport with your listeners?

Before you can improve as a presenter, you must know where you need to correct. After you have done this, concentrate on the techniques outlined in this book and you will become better.

Acknowledge your strengths and use them to your advantage. Analyse your weaknesses and work on them. Focus your energy and time on bringing confidence, impact and polish to what you have to say.

## Does Practice Make Perfect?

There are four stages through which we pass to learn a new skill: unconscious incompetence, conscious incompetence, conscious competence, and unconscious competence - these are highlighted on the accompanying chart.

Having purchased this book you probably aren't an unconscious incompetent! However, you might be a conscious incompetent or a conscious competent. Many presenters remain unconscious incompetents. Unfortunately, they are the ones who need to improve their skills the most, and they didn't buy this book!

Very few people are unconscious competents - this means that they can give excellent presentations without thinking about what they are doing.

The problem with being an unconscious competent is that it is easy to fall unexpectedly down the stairs to unconscious incompetence!

These people might be company Presidents or gurus of the industry and nobody dare tell them how bad they are!

Always be aware of where you are. This way, you will have more control over yourself and your presentation.

*When you're green*
*you grow.*
*When you're ripe*
*you rot!*

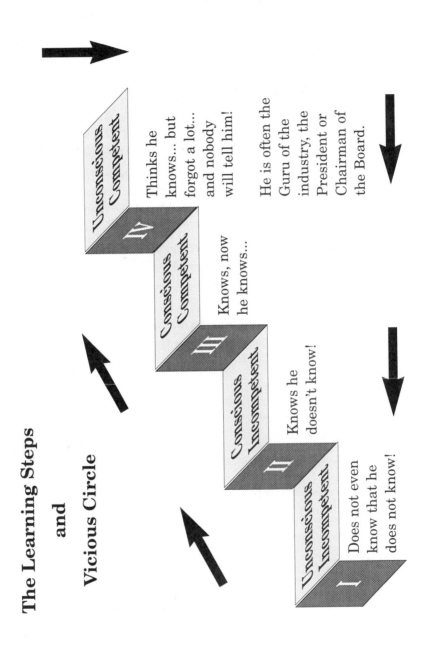

**The Learning Steps and Vicious Circle**

IV — Unconscious Competent
Thinks he knows... but forgot a lot... and nobody will tell him!

He is often the Guru of the industry, the President or Chairman of the Board.

III — Conscious Competent
Knows, now he knows...

II — Conscious Incompetent
Knows he doesn't know!

I — Unconscious Incompetent
Does not even know that he does not know!

# Remember When You Learned to Walk?

When we acquire a new skill or perform a task for the first time, there is an initial start-up period during which the amount of effort we put in far exceeds the results gained.

This happens when learning to ride a bicycle, going on a diet, or learning to speak in public. In the beginning it is a real struggle and the results are minimal.

Most people give up after the first or second try. Very few last beyond three attempts. All it takes is one bad speech or one shaky impression and a lot of us chicken out! Some never try again.

However, we all eventually learned to walk. The reason we did is that we just kept trying and falling down until we finally succeeded. Nobody with a normal mind ever stops a child trying to walk because they fall on the floor a few times!

The problem with being an adult is that the risks of failure seem too great for us to be willing to take chances. We are often afraid of what others will think of us if we look foolish. For this reason many never try to become better presenters.

They abandon their goal because of concern with what others will think of them should they fail.

> *Our greatest glory*
> *is not in never falling,*
> *but in rising every time we fall.*
>
> — *Confucius*

# CONFIDENCE

There's no question about it - making an effective presentation does require self-confidence. One must work to develop greater belief in oneself and the ideas being presented. The benefits of greater confidence go far beyond developing improved communication skills.

Self-confidence is what prepares you to take on new and greater challenges in your company and pursue new career opportunities for yourself. The confidence required for a powerful business presentation is a means to an end as well as an end in itself.

In many years of teaching public speaking to all kinds of different folks, I have found that everyone looks more confident than they feel. People (99%) are nervous when they present the first time. Yet, with practice they feel more self-assured and develop more poise.

In my classes, students' perceptions of themselves and each other were tested at the beginning of the course and then after 14 weeks of weekly presentations.

Each student received positive and negative feedback from me, as well as from the entire class after every presentation they made. Here are the results:

## Differences in the Perceived Confidence of Public Speakers

| | After 1st Presentation | After 14th Week |
|---|---|---|
| Looked confident | 75% | 99% |
| Felt confident | 5% | 65% |
| Was nervous just before presenting | 99% | 99% |

# Ways to Improve Your Confidence While Presenting

- When you are being introduced, smile and glance at the audience and then at the person saying all those nice things about you. Do not look down in modesty. Be proud!

- Start very slowly, with your shoulders back and chin up. Then gradually speed up.

- Open your presentation by saying something genuine like:
  "I am glad to be here today..."
  "I am happy to be talking to you about..."
  "I am delighted to share with you...."

- Recognize that you know more about your topic than any of your listeners. You are an expert.

- Wear your best clothes.

- Above all, have a smile on your face. Your body should feel positive too. Keep telling yourself how good you feel.

## Talk to Yourself

Self-talk is very effective in helping you to feel positive and confident as you make your presentation. How you feel is everything in life. What you think determines how you feel and how you feel determines how confident you are. Try saying this to yourself as regularly as you can:

**This will be my best presentation yet. I know more than anyone else in the group. They need my input and everyone will benefit from what I have to say.**

*The most vital quality*
*a speaker can possess*
*is self-assurance!*

*— Peter Urs Bender*

# There Is Nothing For Nothing In Life

If you want to give powerful, impressive presentations, you have to show determination, develop great self-discipline, and invest a tremendous amount of time in preparation. The best speakers all became good the hard way: they have spoken to many, often hundreds, of audiences on the same topic. In the process, they probably made many embarrassing mistakes. Their ability to conquer fear and failure helped them learn from these mistakes.

People who are not afraid of making mistakes learn very quickly. Fear does not hold them back. They are not anxious about potential failure. They know that the risk of misfortune and the embarrassment they endure is far exceeded by the benefits they gain from new experiences.

Good speakers are eager to try out new ideas in front of unknown audiences. Surprisingly enough, when they make a few mistakes no one notices! All the listeners see is the professionalism and sincerity of the confident speaker doing his or her best to communicate. So do not worry about confidence. You already have more than you think you do!

**In presenting, you are judged not
by who you are
but
by who you seem to be.
Aim to be what you want to be:
confident and prepared.**

Think of the best presenter you know right now. The probability is 95% that he or she started at the same point you did! Do the best you can and keep learning. Your sincerity and determination will automatically help you improve.

# Make Mistakes and Learn From Them

The practical presentation skills I suggest in this book, once integrated into your own style, will result in the best performance. But it will take time. So set realistic expectations for yourself.

> *It is more important*
> *to do the Right Thing than*
> *to do the Thing Right!*
>
> — *Peter F. Drucker*

It is of greater benefit to focus on the right things in your presentation than on trying to do every little thing right. It is critical that you focus all of your effort on a few basics, namely: the Speech, Body Language, Equipment, Environment and Preparation.

What opportunities do you have in the next month to make a presentation? Here is a possible list to get you started:

Where to Practice Your Presentation Skills:

- Office staff meetings
- Professional association meetings
- Break-out sessions at conferences
- Service club meetings
- Board meetings
- Trade show presentations
- Night school course presentations
- Weddings, anniversaries, or retirement receptions
- Town hall meetings

Volunteer to present wherever you can. The suggestions listed are opportunities we all have to "say a few words" in front of an audience. What is your outlook toward speaking on these occasions? Can you change your attitude from reluctance and maybe even fear, to enthusiasm and confidence in confronting a new challenge and sharing your ideas with others?

## Be Positive About Presenting

I know that you already have a positive outlook (or you would not be reading this book). I suggest that you apply this attitude to speaking as well. Think of the next gathering where you can make a personal contribution. Use the ideas and techniques in this book in preparation for the best presentation you have ever given.

Be enthusiastic. Be open minded. Be persistent. The skills of powerful presenting will be with you throughout your working and social life, into retirement.

Don't apologize. Do not say at the beginning or during your speech "I don't want to bore you with statistics, but..." or "Sorry, I don't want to take too much of your time, but..."

> *Life is either a daring adventure or nothing.*
> — *Helen Keller*

☞    Share the ideas in this book with a friend: ask them to evaluate your presentation as per checklist on page 225.

*Whatever you can do,*
*or dream you can . . .*
*begin it.*
*Boldness has genius,*
*power and magic in it.*

—*Goethe*

*Success does not come to
those who wait -
and it does not wait
for anyone to come to it.*

*— Anonymous*

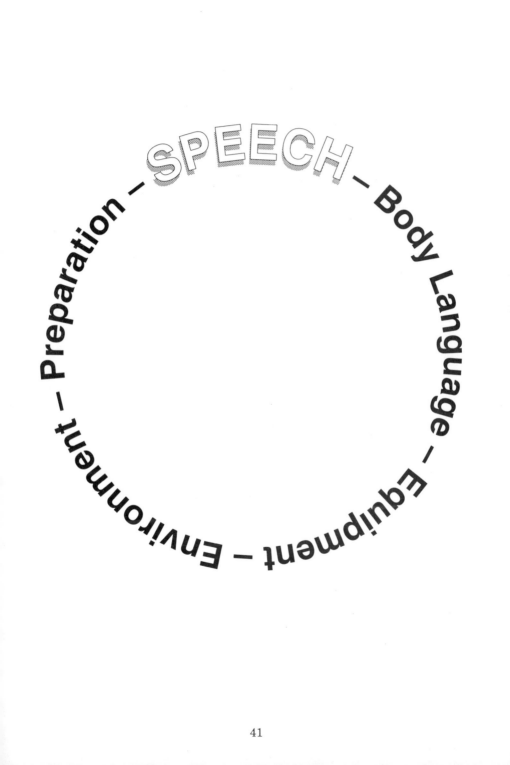

*Is it not strange that we
fear most that which
never happens?
That we destroy our
initiative by the fear of
defeat, when, in reality
defeat is a most useful tonic
and should be accepted
as such.*

*— Napoleon Hill*

# THE FIRST ESSENTIAL:

# THE SPEECH

The content of your presentation is important. Yet, it is not only *what* you say that makes the difference, it is *how* you present it that determines if and how your message will come across. Understanding is the test of effective communication. If your concept is not grasped, *you* did not do a good job.

## Content

It is unfortunate that the way we communicate often distorts what we are trying to say. Your topic is not everything. It is what you do with it that really counts. There are some exceptions of course. Some presentations do succeed in spite of the poorest techniques. You can announce a 20% raise or two extra weeks vacation for your staff and they will not care how you do it! You can do a terrible job and they will still love you. The power of certain messages is sometimes enough in itself. However, most of the time, the way you say it determines whether you will be understood and have your ideas accepted.

## Concurrency

You have to believe whole-heartedly in your message. If you do not, it will show. Let us assume that head office asks you to explain to your people that every department in the company must remain open 30 minutes more per day, but you do not agree. You have a choice: Do not present, change your mind, or resign. Remember: "Lead, follow, or get the hell out". Do not talk to your staff until you are in harmony with the topic.

# Your Presentation Objectives

What is the message you want to convey? What are your objectives in talking to your audience? What knowledge or experience do you have that can benefit people?

An effective presentation demands that you market your topic and yourself. You have to sell your ideas and yourself to the audience.

To be a successful presenter, you must develop an approach which addresses the listeners' interests as specifically and personally as possible.

Your presentation may not always seem, at first glance, to benefit your audience and may even seem threatening to them. Sometimes you will need to present ideas that are more important to the corporation than to the personal interests of the listener.

Often in life there is a difference between what we want to do and what we must do. You may find yourself having to present concepts people do not want to hear at all. The challenge then rests in finding a benefit for your audience – admittedly no easy task – but possible.

**A speech has to have at least one of four objectives:**

- **to inform,**
- **to entertain,**
- **to touch the emotions,**
- **to move to action.**

**A good presentation covers all four objectives.**

Next time you watch TV, pay close attention to the different communication objectives met by the program you are watching.

As a presentation, it must have at least one of four objectives: to inform, to entertain, to touch the audience's emotions, or to move them to action. Usually television focuses on entertainment. But if it doesn't involve any one of the four objectives, you are wasting your time!

## To Inform

This is the most common objective. When you inform, you are sharing knowledge. You are providing news which should be interesting and helpful. Be careful to talk only about data that is relevant to the audience's needs or wants.

Try not to waste time explaining ideas they do not care about. And remember, too much information is deadly. People can absorb only so much. If they become overwhelmed you have lost them.

Do not place too much emphasis on one particular presentation objective to the detriment of others. Decide what is essential and leave out the rest. Interested listeners can always ask you for more details later.

However, if you do not provide your audience with enough information during the presentation, your credibility and competence will soon be questioned. The audience will be unable to act the way you want it to.

Listeners must have sufficient facts to make a favorable decision or your efforts will have been wasted.

# To Entertain

This is the toughest thing to do! I highly recommend that you refrain from telling jokes. There is always the risk of offending someone no matter how careful you are. The delivery and punch line must be perfect or you will look like a fool. If you omit an important part of the joke and it doesn't make sense, people will not laugh and you may be quite embarrassed.

People often tell jokes or funny stories that have nothing to do with the presentation. If you have a talent for humor these can be great starters. However, even if they are entertaining, you may waste the audience's time if you overdo them. Always relate your humor directly to your presentation topic.

I believe that the best and safest humor is a story or anecdote from your own personal experience. It is better to throw eggs at yourself than at others. If you do it this way, it does not matter whether the audience laughs or not. Because you are telling a fable from your own experience, there is no risk that you will not do it right. If you forget any details, no one will notice!

Personal anecdotes and self-deprecating humor are the most sincere way to win an audience over. They will trust you more if you poke fun at yourself and laugh at your faults or failures. If you do not think you have any, just ask your spouse or closest friends.

Be sure that you pace the delivery of your humorous material so that the listeners will have enough time to digest it. If you do not pause so the punch line can be absorbed, they will miss your message.

Furthermore, the delay in their laughter will interrupt you as you move on to your next point! Worse still is your attempt to tell several jokes in rapid succession. Many otherwise entertaining presenters miss the mark, because the audience does not hear the punch lines. If you outline a funny anecdote, laugh at it yourself - even if you have told it hundreds of times and do not find it amusing any more! By doing so, you'll be signalling your listeners to react. Most groups are passive until the speaker prompts some release of tension.

Be sure to give enough time for lingering laughter, or it will cut off the beginning of your next lines. React to your own message clearly and obviously and the audience will react in turn. Smile and they will too.

When entertaining be careful that you have a constructive purpose. It is fun to tell jokes and win laughter but the presentation will seem to be a waste of time if there are no concrete results. Try to weave some practical objective into your presentation that your audience can use.

The best approach is to focus on energizing them in the first five to seven minutes of the presentation. Begin with a funny personal experience related to an area of interest, then move into the "meat" of the presentation.

## Touch the Audience's Emotions

Help your audience get in touch with their emotions: make them cry and create a small lump in their throats. If you want to make people cry, cry yourself. If you convey your emotions sincerely, your audience will react and feel the same way you do. If you get choked up, so will they.

However, getting emotional during a presentation is risky. I recommend that you wait at least 12 to 18 months after a negative personal experience, before talking about it in front of a group. This will ensure that you do not lose control when recalling it.

Professional speakers rehearse their material for hours to get their timing right. Be sure that you prepare as well.

Whether you plan to laugh or cry, know what you intend to do in advance. I suggest that you use laughter at the beginning and emotion in the middle.

The early part of the presentation is when you are warming up the audience. Start on a light note and get progressively more serious and personal.

Help the audience feel good about what you have said. End on a positive note. A good presentation should follow the "MMFG-AM" formula: "Make Me Feel Good About Myself". People need to be reassured that they are good human beings, that they are in control of their lives and able to cope with life's challenges.

A responsible speaker will never leave the listeners feeling helpless and hopeless. Do not depress them. Never criticize without offering constructive solutions. Offer ideas to make the situation better.

## MOVE THEM TO ACTION!

Most business people making presentations have to persuade others to do something they are not currently doing. In developing your message in a presentation, ask yourself, what is the one thing you want the audience to do in reaction to your speech?

Do you want your employees to accept a new company philosophy?

Do you want the audience to buy your product or service?

Do you want your head office to approve the expense of a powerful "Presentations Seminar"?

Do you want the committee to vote "Yes" for your new idea or project?

Do you want the personnel committee to promote you?

Write out the *call-to-action* in the form of a question you will ask at the end of your presentation. Be specific and direct. You have to request a commitment! Here are some examples:

Say to each member of your department:

*"If there is one thing we can do to improve our service, what would it be? Please answer this questionnaire and return it to me by Friday."*

*"Call your ten largest customers and ask them what can be done to improve our product. Then let's compare notes and build a new strategy."*

*"If all our managers could make better presentations we would save a lot of frustration and money - Let's get Bender in!"*

The only time you can be "teachy, preachy" is in your call to action. If you do not explicitly request a response from the audience, they will probably wonder what your purpose was. If you do not tell them exactly what to do in reaction to your message no changes will occur and they will forget everything you said and all your efforts will be wasted.

*Great works are performed,*
*not by strength,*
*but by perseverance*

*— Samuel Johnson*

# Communicate In The Same Language As Your Audience

Adjust your vocabulary to suit each particular group to which you present. If they are shareholders, bankers, or accountants and your topic is leveraged buyouts, you require a different vocabulary than if you are talking to marketing people or account executives on strategic selling.

Each audience has its own unique language, familiar expressions and sense of humor with which you must be comfortable or you will not gain credibility.

Be careful of semantics. The words you use will have different connotations in different contexts. The same expression can be specifically or vaguely defined. Some words are used in relative terms and others are absolute, such as large, small, wide, long, easy, difficult, liberal, conservative, ethnic, religious, expensive, cheap – it depends on how you use them. Use meanings that are familiar to your audience. If necessary, explain your own definitions.

For example, "politics" can refer to our system of government, in which there are political parties, or it can refer to the power dynamics between people or departments in a company. "Values" can refer to the company's mission statement, or the particular beliefs of individuals.

In a sales presentation, there is a world of difference between mentioning that a product is "cheap" or saying it is "inexpensive" and "affordable". Different professions and industrial sectors use different euphemisms.

For example, sales people are often titled "account executives", "account managers", "associates", or "product representatives", even "technical consultants" rather than simply "salespeople".

Recruiters sometimes call themselves "executive search consultants", "human resource consultants", or "headhunters". I recommend that you use jargon only with appropriate groups.

Make use of vivid, expressive words that paint pictures the audience can see. Abstract concepts like "recession", "restructuring", "corporate culture", "revenue enhancement" and "free trade" are not as clear as "happy customers", job losses", "plant closings", and "profit after tax". Examine your everyday speech and look for vague expressions that you can replace with more direct and explicit ones. Don't go on talking about "rationalizing your departmental budget" when you really mean you are "cutting costs"!

## The Right Vocabulary

It is possible to be fully understood in any language with only a few hundred words. You may not sound too bright, but you can survive. There is a saying that goes, "When you travel, having a lot of money and a few native words guarantees a great time." This is true wherever you might be visiting, provided you have the money!

There are over 750,000 words in the English language - far more than we can ever learn, let alone use! A high school student has command of about 2,000 words, a university student: 5,000. However, in everyday language, the average business person uses only about 1,000 words.

For a presentation, you must have a vocabulary extensive enough to feel confident and articulate in front of your audience. Moreover, throwing around sophisticated terminology and elaborate phraseology is not always an advantage!

*I rarely think in words at all*

*— Albert Einstein*

51

# Familiar Language Builds Rapport and Trust

Professional presenters know that one key to acceptance and respect is to look, talk, and act the way the audience does. This creates familiarity and builds trust. If you use familiar words and concepts, everyone will be more interested and attentive. They will be more open to your way of thinking. This is especially important when speaking about a controversial topic.

**Don't** talk to your audience in a manner which creates unnecessary distance.

**Don't** talk down to them by using sophisticated words, foreign expressions or obscure quotations, unless you are sure they'll appreciate them.

**Don't** come across as arrogant in your knowledge of your subject and its terminology. Communicate to listeners in language that they can understand.

If you address a technical or academic group, you should use their precise buzzwords. If they tend to be very serious, you could lighten them up by using more colorful language. Your aim is to be understood and that becomes much easier when the audience accepts you.

*In the right key
one can say anything.
In the wrong key
nothing:
The only delicate part is
the establishment of the key.*

— *George Bernard Shaw*

## Use Shorter Words and Phrases

The most powerful words in our language tend to be short. For example: love, war, sex, food, hate, fun, money, power. If a sentence is so lengthy that you have to stop to take a breath, it will be too long to be understood. Break long sentences and phrases into shorter ones. What words can you eliminate to clean up your speech? Do they cloud or clarify the message you are trying to convey? Work on this in your daily business correspondence and it will automatically rub off in your speech.

## What's In It For Me?

We all process new information when forming opinions or making decisions. Usually this is done on the basis of self interest. We all listen to the same radio station - WII-FM: "What's In It For Me?". The truly effective presenter can convey rewards to the audience and uses every opportunity to demonstrate those benefits in the presentation.

> *You must earn the right to speak!*
> — *Dale Carnegie*

Most of the time, having enthusiasm, a purpose and a sense of the interests of the audience are all that you need to make an effective presentation. Be sincere as you attempt to relate to your listeners. Do not ever bluff or pretend that you have things in common with them if you really don't. They will see it. Be honest and emphasize areas of genuine commonality. If you cannot see any, keep looking.

# Some Popular Audience
# AM and FM Radio Stations

| | |
|---|---|
| **LMFO - FM** | "Let me find out for myself" |
| **MMFG - AM** | "Make me feel good about myself" |
| **WII - FM** | "What's in it for me?" |
| **MMFI - AM** | "Make me feel important about myself" |
| **HCIB - FM** | "How can I benefit for myself?" |
| **SSI - AM** | "Show some interest addressing me" |
| **GMB - FM** | "Give me benefits for me!" |
| **MMFC - AM** | "Make me feel confident about myself" |
| **ITOI - FM** | "Is this of interest for me?" |

## Selecting The Presentation Topic

Everyone loves a presenter who doesn't go on too long.

*A speech should be like a woman's skirt:*
*Long enough to cover the topic yet*
*short enough to be interesting.*

*— Winston Churchill*

Be sure that you have enough material for the length of your talk - but not too much! Never try to cover too many things or you will not hold your audience's attention. Keep your message as simple as possible. Repeat your central point several times and in different ways.

After considering the interests of your listeners, decide quickly what your topic will be and immediately start researching what you will cover. Make the subject as broad as your audience. If they are specialists from the same profession, focus on precise points you know they'll want to hear about. If they represent a cross-section of the general public, make it as broad as possible. Explain the basic points that will be unfamiliar to some participants. If you are preparing your presentation to be given more than once before different groups, be as general as possible. Then, tailor the presentation to each specific situation as the need arises.

If you are an expert or a near-expert on your topic, the content as it relates to your audience should be obvious. Your task is to organize and summarize the material into manageable bites that can be digested easily in a 30 to 60 minute talk. The rule here is "less is more".

Be passionate about your topic and thoroughly knowledgeable. You will feel highly confident and no one will be able to stump you with a question. Pay attention to what your colleagues and other managers and executives are saying in the subject area. Read business papers, journals and newsletters to get new ideas. What is missing that you can possibly improve? Ask others for input you can use in your presentation.

# Organize Your Presentation

It is usually not very difficult to find enough material for a speech. The hard part is deciding how to put it all together. There are an infinite number of perspectives on any single topic and any one of them might be appropriate for a particular audience.

## Have an Idea File

Your topic should be thoroughly researched. Keep an idea file solely devoted to your presentations. Save clippings, quotations and magazine articles in it. Have a separate one for each topic you might want to present. If you give many presentations on more than one topic you may want to develop a more sophisticated system for cataloguing your ideas.

You should have much more material than you can cover in your talk. In order to be an authority in front of your audience, you should know at least ten times as much about your topic as they do. Then you are an expert in their eyes.

Collect personal anecdotes that show you at your creative best. Think also of times when you made mistakes. Be prepared to talk about how you learned life's lessons. Can you remember the times when you made a fool of yourself? Can you laugh at yourself now? Turn these experiences into positive stories. Your audience will appreciate your sincerity. Think about what you learned. Record your ideas on 3 x 5 notecards and keep them in your idea file.

# Develop a Catchy Title

Choosing a good title will give you focus as you prepare and it will arouse the interest of others prior to the event. Think of a "grabber" that is short, vivid, easy to say, original and memorable.

One way to do this is to write out your mission statement and then reduce it to the key words. Soon you will end up with a unique and powerful title.

Develop several alternatives and ask others for their preference. Keep making changes until you arrive at one that pleases and excites everyone.

# Mapping Your Presentation Outline

A great way to begin organizing your presentation is to "map" your ideas determining how they relate to each other. If you are new to presenting (or to a certain topic area) the outline of your message may not be readily apparent.

A map will help you to determine which are the essential or primary points to cover and which are secondary.

- Start with the topic written in the centre of a blank page.
- What related issues come to mind? Write them down. Draw lines connecting each related word to the center.
- For each new word, think of related key words and draw connecting lines. Be inclusive rather than exclusive.
- Write down as many related key words as you can to ensure that you haven't missed anything.

The value of mapping is that it helps you to visualize abstract, complex topics and their related concepts. It also helps you to make choices concerning your talk. You can always cut out material if you have too much.

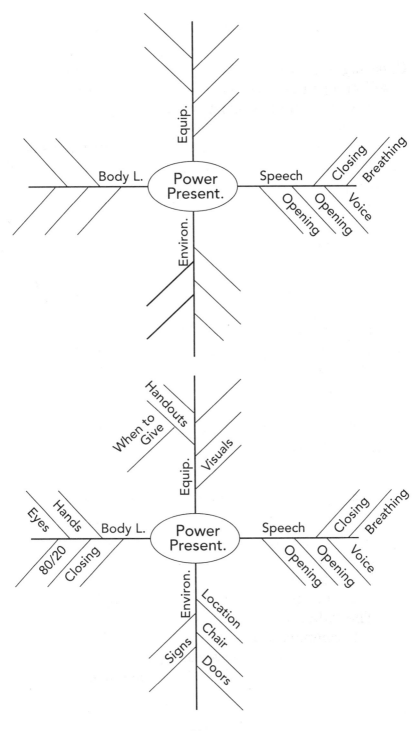

# Use Small Notecards to Organize Your Speech

Another very useful technique is to write all ideas related to your topic on 3" x 5" file cards, using one per idea.

Once you have done this, arrange and rearrange the cards determining the best order for you in the presentation of your points. Experiment with different sequences. When are satisfied with the flow, number your points and on you go!

# The Right Structure: Have Three to Seven Points

It is always best to keep your structure as simple as possible. You will not want too many main points, nor too many sub-points. Aim for no more than three, although for a longer presentation you might have up to seven. Your audience will not remember any more ideas than that anyway.

Start with the simplest and most general concepts, then progress to your more specific and complicated ones. Ease into it so you will not lose your listeners.

Develop a structure which can be easily memorized by you and your listeners, such as "our five key markets", "seven elements of successful leadership", "six components of effective time management", or "three ways to increase our sales".

Your presentation approach might involve the discussion of events in chronological order – past, present, future. Or it might be organized around geographical proximity – near, semi-distant, far.

You could talk about different categories of ideas – apples, oranges, bananas – or a sequence or hierarchy of conceptual steps - first, second, and third.

Just remember, there is no right way to organize your presentation. The main thing is the development of structure.

Otherwise, you will stumble all over the map – and the Chairman of the Board is the only one allowed to do that!

# Possible Methods of Structuring Your Presentation

- **Chronological/Historical: Past, Present, Future**

- **Sequential: First, Second, Third**

- **Geographical: North, South, East, West**

- **Categorical: Oranges, Apples, Bananas, Pineapples; or: Triangles, Circles, Squares, Rectangles; or: Customers, Managers, Employees, Sales People**

- **Compare and Contrast Extremes: Negative versus Positive; "Go Ahead Now" versus "Think About It"; "Our side" versus "Their side"**

- **Hierarchical: Top, Middle, Bottom**

- **Review Options: Option 1, Option 2, Option 3, Recommendation**

- **Expanding Radius: Individual, Neighbourhood, Community**

Because there is no right or wrong way to structure your presentation, avoid spending too much time trying to determine which is best. It is better to decide as soon as possible to go with an approach you feel is workable and then concentrate on practicing your delivery.

There will always be another way you could have done it. If absolutely necessary, you can change ideas here and there as you prepare. But it is important to make a choice and move on in the preparation of your presentation.

**Many presentations fail
because people try too hard
to achieve perfection
in the content of their speech
as opposed to spending time
rehearsing the delivery of the message.**

*There are two things people want
more than sex and money...
Recognition and Praise*

*— Mary Kay Ash*

# The 80/20 Rule

You should spend eighty percent of your preparation time on delivery and only twenty percent on determining the content of your speech. Sound surprising? Not really. Because you are already an expert on your topic, the outline and relevant points you present should be fairly obvious to you.

However, a confident and professional presentation style will take some effort. Do not spend all of your time on content. Work not on what you will say as much as how you will say it. If you are not 100% familiar with your topic, though, the proportion of time required to master content must increase.

# Writing a Draft

Define your purpose, assemble ideas, facts, anecdotes, and statistics around your topic and develop your outline. For first time presenters only, you might want to develop a draft of your speech, including key phrases that you find particularly effective. Do this even if you intend to speak without notes.

Writing a draft will help you to clarify your ideas and the style in which you will convey them. Do not worry about perfection. Not yet!

Write your draft as quickly as possible and revise it later. The point is to get all of your ideas down so that you can analyze and refine them. While many of the world's most famous speeches were given extemporaneously, eloquence is guaranteed if you prepare the *thoughts* you will use in advance.

# Rehearse By Reading Your Draft Aloud

Read aloud through your draft several times, looking for phrases that can be improved and big words that can be replaced with simpler, less pretentious ones. Use the same vocabulary as your audience.

Do not be long winded. Say as much as you can in as few words as possible. Watch repetition. Sometimes it's effective but most often it's annoying. Be careful about the word "I" and statements like "I did", "I think", "I will". Instead emphasize "we" and "you" as much as possible.

Practice reading your draft at a normal rate of speech – about 145 words per minute. You'll get a feel for how to emphasize certain expressions and phrases, how to breathe, and where to pause.

One thing, though, is true: you will tend to speak faster before an audience than during rehearsal. Fit the speed of your delivery to the listeners. If it consists mostly of older people, speak more slowly. If they are younger, you can speed up a bit.

# Conviction

For your presentation to succeed, you must believe whole-heartedly in your message. If you do not, it will be obvious. It takes a very skillful presenter – or actor for that matter – to convincingly give a false presentation. If you are truly convinced of the value of your mission, and you genuinely feel that your ideas can help the audience, be sure to show it!

# Monitor The Audience's Reaction

When presenting, everything you do and everything you say may be received differently by members of your audience. Your message will not come across successfully unless you are sending the right signals. Constantly monitor your audience as you present. Obtain feedback as often as possible and make needed adjustments. If faces look puzzled, pause and ask if you have been clear. If not, try to say it another way. Listen to their reaction to your material. If they do not laugh at your jokes, ease up on the humor and be more serious.

If there is anything that seems wrong as you begin your presentation, or if people seem clearly distracted, stop immediately to rectify the situation.

Also, be sensitive to what has happened immediately prior to your presentation that day. Be aware if there has been a recent tragedy, controversial company policy, or political or personal conflict that might be distracting the audience. Do not open it up for discussion but be aware of it.

## Help the Audience Understand You

Repeating your point several times in different ways throughout the presentation helps your audience understand you better. Reinforce your message with visual aids.

Specifically, tell your listeners how they can act on the information you have given them to do their jobs better. Obtaining periodic feedback from them will also lead to successful understanding.

## READING A PREPARED SPEECH

I strongly advise that you *not* read your speech from a text. However, there still might be a time when you will want to use a written speech. This could be when you are presenting in another language, during a highly technical session where you want to ensure accurate information, or when you are making a statement of very important facts at a press conference.

Think of the last time you heard someone read a speech. It probably was boring. The reason? The speaker's attention was concentrated on correctly reading the words in the text.

This restraines the speaker's body language. The brain concentrates on the text rather than allowing the body to express itself naturally.

However, if you insist on reading a speech, print your text in large, triple-spaced type. You can also enlarge the text using the enlargement feature on your photocopier. Use only the top two thirds of the page so that when you rest it on the lectern your eyes will not have to look down quite so far.

Indent all lines *after* the first line of each paragraph – this is the opposite of what you see in books. The opening sentences will stand out. Avoid splitting sentences or paragraphs over two pages. Put several periods at the end of each sentence to indicate pauses – otherwise your eyes will confuse the periods with commas.

When referring to numbers, do not spell them out unless you are talking about round numbers like "hundred", "thousand", "million", etc. For figures, use numerals e.g. 1,243,864. Spell out "dollars", "percent", "degrees Celsius", and other common symbols.

As you read through each page, *do not* turn it over. This distracts and draws even more attention to the fact that you are reading the speech. Instead, gently slide the sheet to one side as you proceed to the next. Be sure that your pages are numbered in the top right margin. At the bottom of each page, note the first few words of the page following.

Make note of all breath and emphasis marks right in the text of the speech.

Also, if a phrase is to be accompanied by a particular gesture or expression, make a note in the text.

If you must remind yourself to smile – or frown – draw a small face on the page. Or, use colors like red to emphasize certain words.

Put instructions in brackets, reminding yourself when to use visual aids and when to distribute handouts. I also suggest that you note appropriate times to make eye contact with your listeners.

Above all, you *must* rehearse when you plan to read your speech. The reason so many speakers are incredibly boring is that they stumble through their unrehearsed speeches without energy and polish. Most of the time, speeches read from a text sound sloppy. A prepared speaker who takes the time to practice reading aloud through the text a few times, can deliver with enthusiasm and energy to capture the interest and attention of the audience.

*Do not hide behind the lectern*

Another disadvantage of reading a speech, especially if you do not have a lectern, is that your nervousness will tend to be more obvious to the audience. They will see your hands shaking as you hold the pages. There may also be a risk that poor lighting will make it difficult to read the text. To be on the safe side, bring your own little flashlight. It could save you some embarrassing moments. There are even clip-on types which are quite effective for speakers.

If, by accident, you read the same sentence twice, you may get rattled and lose your concentration. So be careful when you read your speech! Rehearse it. If you think you have no time, you are wrong. There is always the taxi ride to the airport, or a few moments in the restroom.

*Again, **I do not** recommend that anyone – even a first-time presenter – should stand behind a lectern and read a speech, unless your presentation is in another language. But if you do anyway, please, practice, practice, practice!*

# Minimal Notes: Using 4" x 6" Cards

This is a far better method than writing your speech out completely. Yet it still provides you with some security in case you lose your place.

The 4" x 6" notecards marked with key words will trigger your memory. They might be the best way for you to avoid forgetting important points, just as they are for many well-known presenters.

Your use of note cards will also make you look professional. When the audience sees cards in your hands they assume that you have planned out what you want to say! Don't have more than six or seven, whether you are speaking for three minutes, thirty minutes, or an hour.

Cards are highly recommended because they force you to think on your feet and use your body naturally to express your message. An experienced speaker, having given a talk many times can usually write all of the notes on a single card. One word will simply trigger entire sections of the presentation.

Write out your opening and closing in full on one card each. This is very important. Your mind is standard equipment and will work well for you most of the time – except when you are addressing a large group!

With cards, if you lose your place or forget your closing, at least you have it written in front of you. This guarantees that you will always be on target and your beginning and summary statements will be clearly communicated to your audience.

Be sure to number your cards on the top right. Speakers who do not do this are greatly embarrassed when they drop them. Often they also shuffle them like a deck of cards just before beginning!

Use different colors to emphasize certain points and gestures. Mark your cards with special symbols telling you when to change your body language, vocal tone and pacing.

Use key words only, with the exception of quotations and opening and closing statements.

Be thoroughly familiar with your notes and the markings in them. You should know the content so well that you won't need to refer too much to your cards. You will have them just to glance at and ensure that you do not miss anything.

Your markings should instantly trigger recall of the points you want to make. Do not look nervously at your notes and talk at the same time.

Instead, quickly scan your card, then look up, smile and convey your ideas from memory. Develop a smooth cycle whereby your eyes move over the note cards to the audience.

When speaking in a large room where you will shift around quite a bit, you could plant note cards in various places to help keep you on track. If you intend to use a blackboard, place one on the chalk ledge with all of the points to be written on the board. Doing this will also give you a good reason to move, thus enhancing your body language.

If you are concerned about going overtime, place extra note cards in your deck marked with reminders to look at the clock.

## "Brown-outs"

Every speaker has experienced times when they temporarily lost their place or forgot an important thought in mid-sentence. Accept this as natural.

The way to minimize brown-outs is to prepare in advance and becoming thoroughly familiar with a few important key points rather than many. The details will automatically follow when the main points are clearly etched in your mind.

But even with preparation you still might experience a situation where you suddenly do not know where you are, what you said or what is next! Do not panic.

Inexperienced speakers typically do the following during a brown-out: they suddenly realize they are lost; panic strikes; they signal messages of great discomfort; they bite their lips, lower them a bit, tilt their head down and put on their most defensive look. The audience wakes up and everybody in the room notices that the speaker is lost!

You, however, will be different. You simply smile and go on to the next card. Not the one in front of you, but the one following. Look at the first word on it. This will be the point from which you will now continue. Just move on.

Of course you missed part of your speech. So what? Just follow my techniques – cheerfully, with a smile – and nobody but you will notice! Your audience will blame themselves for not following your thoughts. They will think they should not have had so much to drink the night before. Or they will blame themselves for day dreaming! Almost certainly, they will think that it is their fault!

## Why Use Notecards?

- They are more convenient and less obvious than 8.5 by 11 inch paper
- They prevent embarrassment from brown-outs
- They make you look prepared and polished
- They encourage you to think on your feet

# Tips for Using 4" x 6" Notecards

- **Key words only. Less is more!**

- **Write out your opening and closing lines in full on two separate cards**

- **Number them clearly in the upper right hand corner**

- **Handprint or type your notes using upper and lower case letters**

- **Mark your cards with colors and symbols indicating instructions for visual aids, body language, etc.**

- **Use no more than seven cards for a single presentation**

## Let Your Visuals Be Your Notes

If you use several overhead transparencies, flipcharts, slides or handouts (see Page 146 on Equipment) during your presentation you really do not need note cards. Your key words will already be there on the visuals.

When presenting, just look at them and then at the audience. This will help your body language as well. You will appear a lot more natural glancing at a flipchart than looking down at your cards.

This approach will keep you thinking on your feet and will still provide security if something goes wrong.

## TelePrompter

Be sure you do a trial run... I suggest you go through the entire speach first without an audience. Practice, practice, practice.

## A Presentation Is Like A Flight

It has a take-off and a landing - an opening and a closing. In between, there may be some turbulence or rough riding. But, just like a flight, as long as you take off and land smoothly and safely, your presentation is a success!

If you have kept the attention of your audience, you have succeeded. In the middle, you may make some mistakes.

Some members of the audience might drift away or look like they might fall asleep - never a good sign! Someone might challenge your facts and figures outright.

However, like a pilot, a skillful presenter makes mid-air corrections to stay safely on course. If you slip up, minimize the damage and continue with a smile.

A presentation is judged by how well you met your stated objectives and not by how many mistakes you made. Most of the time, you will be the only one who notices.

# How to Begin Your Speech

Listeners today have very short attention spans. You must capture and hold their interest immediately or it will be hard for you to succeed. As on television, your presentation should contain a series of interesting and provocative "sound bites" one after the other.

# Go From the Familiar to the Unfamiliar

You must first be accepted and trusted by your audience before they will really listen to you. Begin with familiar ideas that you know are already understood and accepted, then build on them. Move from the familiar to the unfamiliar.

In preparation, ask yourself, what do they already know about your topic? Briefly talk about points of common understanding and summarize these before moving on to new material.

Here are some suggestions for an effective "take-off". The sole objective of your opening is to capture and keep the listener's attention, and have them wanting to hear more. Be sure that your opening is specifically tailored for the group and occasion. Create it just for them! Emphasize the listeners rather than yourself.

# Make Them Participants — Not Spectators

Have you ever noticed how many speakers tell us things without explaining their significance? We are left thinking, "What was that supposed to mean?".

Speakers often fail to create a context which would enable listeners to relate to their message. Therefore, always emphasize "You" when communicating, rather than "I" and "Me".

Involve the other person in your message. Your concern for the audience's interest should be obvious by the words used in your presentation. Words such as "we" and "you" involve audiences whereas the use of "I" and "my" exclude them. When explaining things that are not part of an audience's experience, it is important to create a familiar context, enabling them to appreciate the situation being described.

Use phrases like this,

> "Imagine that *you* are in a situation in which..."
> "What would *you* do if...."
> "Assuming that *you* are in a position where...."
> "Imagine that *you* have just...."

Help the audience to visualize the situation with their own eyes. Bring them right into it. Use words that make them participants rather than spectators. Help them feel what you have experienced by using inclusive language. To begin your presentation, use a "hook" which involves your audience in your message as quickly as possible. Spend time preparing the best opening point and choose the most effective communications media - pure speech, physical demonstration, visuals, and audience participation exercises. Here are several "hooks" you can use:

## Tell a Story

Be sincere and make it personal. Talk about yourself. *"A funny thing happened on the way here..."* Just go right into it. Do not say: *"I want to tell you a story"*. The anecdote must relate to the presentation in some way or they will wonder why you are telling it. Have lots of tales saved up in your idea file. Remember, it's best to talk about your personal experiences.

# Acknowledge the Occasion and the Audience

This is effective for special conferences and unique meetings where your listeners will not have been gathered together before. Try these:

*"Today is a very special occasion because..."*

*"This is the first time that we have gathered all of our managers from coast to coast in one room..."*

*"It is especially appropriate that we are talking about computers today because..."*

Your opening statement will indicate how your topic is appropriate for that audience at that particular time.

# Pay the Listeners a Compliment

Be sure that it is genuine. Warm them up. Establish trust:

*"I want to thank all of you for your hospitality last night when I first arrived. You have a reputation for friendliness and now I know why..."*

*"For many years, I have worked with the company's accounting department and I have admired the training your division has provided its employees. Obviously, you're all very good at what you do. My purpose today is to help you to..."*

We are all the same. We appreciate it when someone says something good about us. Always give compliments in the first quarter of your presentation to help build rapport and trust.

# Quotations

Be careful with these. Quotations should be handled well or not at all. Make sure they fit smoothly into your presentation and enhance your message. Never come across as a snob or a know-it-all. Do not use a quotation for the sake of using one. Beware of the fallacy of authority - just because the person you are quoting is famous, or an expert in something, that does not mean that they know something about your topic.

Stick with the acknowledged authorities in your field and quote them only in their area of expertise. It is important to choose sayings from notables the audience will recognize and respect. Pick names that will enhance your credibility and that of your topic. Adolf Hitler will not be perceived as providing words of wisdom for most audiences.

> *Coming together is a beginning;*
> *keeping together is progress;*
> *working together is success.*
> *— Henry Ford*

Quotes are useful because they illustrate that someone has already concisely expressed your message. Having described a concept in your presentation, it is helpful to show the audience that someone has reached the conclusion earlier.

Quotations, in a way, help take the weight off of your shoulders. They are also important if you are referring to ideas from original experts on a subject, such as management theories, employee relations, computer hardware, or the company's founding philosophy. Quotations allow you to tap into the credibility of respected authorities.

Write your quotations in full on separate cards. Better still, bring the book with the page marked and show the audience. Use Post–it notes rather than book marks which have a tendency to fall out just when you are trying to locate the page. Practice reciting the quotation several times in advance. Get the rhythm of the phrasing right for maximum effect. Do not stumble because of lack of practice.

## Make a Striking Statement

Be sure it is true. Make use of dramatic effect. For example:

*"Our company could become the industry leader if we successfully implement the proposal I am about to share with you . . ."*

*"If we continue to waste time at meetings at the rate we are doing, our company will be bankrupt in ten years..."*

The point is to jolt the audience with a new thought, to challenge them to consider something unusual or uncommon, to arouse their curiosity.

## Use an Unusual Statistic

Here is a good example:

*"99.9% is not good enough! A study by the Quality Control Institute of California determined that if we were satisfied with 99.9% accuracy, 22,000 checks would be cashed by the wrong bank every hour, 50 newborn babies would be dropped every day, 500 incorrect surgical operations would take place each week, 20,000 drug prescriptions would be incorrectly*

*filled each year. More significantly, 32,000 heartbeats would be missed in every human heart each year."*

*"If all of our unhappy customers were to hold hands, we would have a chain around the perimeter of a football field..."*

*"If we stacked up all the thank you letters from our customers the pile would be one hundred feet high..."*

*"If we maintain our present profit margin, the company will be bankrupt by..."*

## Refer to a Statement Made by a Preceding Speaker

If you are at a conference or convention and previous speakers said something of relevance to your topic, refer to it. It is always a nice gesture. If you feel that they made an important contribution, compliment them and tell the audience just what you gained from their message. It is important to evaluate the audience reaction. If they liked what the speaker had to say, you have an opportunity to emphasize your own position more strongly. Paying compliments to others is always a class act. For example:

*"Before I begin, I want to comment on what John Smith was saying about the importance of teamwork in our company. The advice he gave you worked very well for me..."* (tell a story illustrating the validity of the previous speaker's point).

# Ask the Audience a Challenging Question

Some examples:

*"How long will it take us to develop a widget which is superior in quality yet lower in price?"*

*"How long, at the present rate will it take before the world's forests are completely depleted?"*

*"What is the single most common cause of business failure today?"*

*"What does each department have to do in order for our company to regain its position as industry leader?"*

In asking a challenging question, be sure that you provide an answer later in your presentation, or you should help the audience find the answer on its own.

# Ask for a Show of Hands

Of course, not everyone will cooperate with you and do this. There is a difference in response between American and British audiences, between extroverts and introverts. Some find this technique childish. However, you will find that most audiences will participate. Ask good relevant questions. Get to know the different groups represented in your audience, where they come from, how many years each person has been with the company and so on. Be sincere and acknowledge their answers. An effective technique for producing a show of hands is to raise your own hand and hold it high above your head. Demonstrate what you ask your audience to do. It is like anything else in management, if you show you are willing to do it yourself, your staff will be more willing.

## Establish Your Believability

If you do not have credibility, no one will listen. Do not ever misrepresent yourself and your experience. Never, ever, lie! The audience will eventually find out. Credibility is hard to gain and easy to lose. References to other speaking engagements completed recently or other audiences' reactions to your suggestions can help establish believability as long as it is not overdone.

For example:

> *"I was speaking to an audience of investment bankers last week in Zurich and one person told me that the most serious concern on his mind these days is the decline of junk bonds..."*

In establishing your believability, you are creating an image of professional competence and experience, by referring to your other activities in business and your contacts. If you tell your audience it will create a positive context for your topic. As a result, they will take your message more seriously.

Another way to establish credibility is to draw attention to a recent personal achievement that the group can relate to, such as a promotion, an award, a report you have written or the publication of an article. Make a statement that somehow indicates that you have experience qualifying you to speak on your topic.

Essentially, try to follow this formula for enhancing the believability of your presentation: two-thirds of your credibility during a presentation should be evident from what you say with the remaining one-third coming from any written materials you hand out or visual aids you use.

## Make a Promise

Be realistic and be sure that you are able to follow through. For example:

*"In the next 20 minutes, I am going to share with you an idea that, if implemented will increase company sales by up to 20%..."*

*"In the next hour, I am going to take you through an exercise that will greatly enhance your customer relations..."*

*"After I finish this seminar, you will all be able to make much better presentations than ever before."*

## Show a Two Minute Video

This could possibly be an introduction of your company, yourself, a statement about the importance of your topic, or a quick summary of the main points of your presentation. It may be expensive to do this but it is worthwhile if you plan to make the same presentation many times to different audiences.

## Start With an Overhead Transparency or Slide

You might consider beginning a discussion with a slide or overhead. The multi-media impact of such a visual at the start will help you capture and hold the listeners' attention.

My favorite slide/overhead reads:

It does not say: Switzerland in the Spring, America in the Fall
... Please read it again ...

## How I Use This Overhead

At the beginning, or during a presentation, the audience is asked to stand up and the projector is turned on. They are instructed to read what appears on the screen.

Then I ask them: "If you read differently than I do, please sit down." I repeat 3-4 times "Switzerland in the Spring, America in the Fall". Most are still standing while I smile and end by reading what is really on the overhead. "Switzerland in the the Spring, America in the the Fall!"

The purpose of this exercise is to remind audiences that we must look at things differently in order to understand. When we get set in our ways of approaching problems, either in business or in our private lives, we miss very important opportunities and ideas. The edge goes to those who can look at themselves, their problems and unresolved issues, from different points of view. Please feel free to use this to prepare an overhead transparency and show it to your management team.

# Switzerland in the the Spring

# America in the the Fall

# Present An Outline

If your topic is particularly detailed and theoretical or if you will be speaking for several hours, develop an outline of your presentation to be shown on a slide or overhead transparency. Begin by explaining the general points you'll cover. Then, at summary intervals in your talk, review the outline indicating how you have been progressing through it. For example, you might say:

> *"This outline provides us with an overview of the plan for the restructuring of Jones Manufacturing. Let's look at all six major divisions in our new company and what is in store for them next year. Each one is charged with five key objectives, which you as managers will be responsible for implementing..."*

> *"We have reviewed three of the five new strategies for improving service: [point to each as you review it on the outline] decentralized product service depots, 800 number customer service hot-lines, and 48 hour guaranteed parts service. Now I will move to the next point: Product focus of our top ten clients...."*

There are many possibilities. As usual, be sure that your opening visual - if you want to use one - has some immediate purpose in getting your presentation started. If you think your topic is too complicated to lend itself to a visual outline, something is wrong with the organization of your talk. The more complicated your talk, the more you should seek to simplify your points. If you do not, the audience will not pay attention and will not retain what you say. Conversely, the less complicated your topic, the more detailed your points can be.

## Get the Audience to Participate During the Presentation

In order to really communicate with your listeners, you need to involve them in your message. Ask them to help with specific parts of your presentation as early as possible. Seek volunteers to demonstrate certain points. Arrange with them in advance. No surprises! You will look like a fool if nobody wants to play with you! Do not call on them unless you have received permission to do so before you start.

Above all, do not embarrass the participants or make them feel foolish in front of their peers. If you do, resentment will build in the audience and you will lose credibility.

## How <u>Not</u> to Begin

Do not be too formal and start with:

> *"Mr. Chairman, Mr. President, Mr. Vice-President, fellow colleagues and honored guests....".*

This is stuffy and unnatural, most of the time. Maybe you heard it at Toastmasters. There it is okay and it was good years ago. Today, it is annoying and a waste of everyone's time.

## Get Someone Else to Introduce You

The listener's perception of your credibility depends on how well you begin. If it looks like you know what you are doing, the audience will lend you their ears right away. It's extremely important that you begin on a smooth, positive note.

Your credibility and believability is much more easily established if you get a strong introduction from someone the audience already knows and respects. It is much better to have others say nice things about you than for you to do it yourself! However, many presentations suffer because of poor introductions. Sometimes the person introducing you is a terrible speaker and says things that are inaccurate, confuusing to the audience, or simply ignorant of your expertise. Some even tell bad, offensive jokes or mention things which undermine the points you will be trying to make in your presentation. This can really hurt your performance and make it hard for you to establish credibility.

The secret of a smooth, effective introduction therefore is to prepare it in advance for the person who will introduce you. It is critical that you provide the introducer with some material to use. I recommend that you supply him with a written introduction which can be read aloud word for word. In this way, they will be saying exactly what you want. Most introducers appreciate this. Be fair and objective about yourself and willing to have them talk about your accomplishments. As long as these are relevant to your topic, they are important to include. Discourage the introducer from ad libbing or changing your prepared text. Explain that the success of your presentation depends on a smooth introduction with the material provided.

If possible, personally select the person who will introduce you. Then, provide them with the prepared introduction that will start your presentation smoothly. Do not pick someone who is known for publicly boosting their own ego. They might talk more about themselves than you!

You will not always have the luxury of picking your introducer. At certain functions, the presiding officer will announce you. At a formal dinner, for example, the chairperson will designate a member to introduce you and another to thank you. Most of the time, the introducer will prepare in advance.

He might contact you to learn more about your background, what you plan to say, and the relevance of your topic to the audience. However, most will wait until the last minute to talk to you. Be pro-active. Find out who will introduce you and contact them at least two days in advance. Get to know them and make them your ally. See Page 197 on Preparation.

## Be Heard!

There is one rule above all others when speaking: Make sure that your audience can hear you! If necessary, use a microphone. There is absolutely no excuse for not being loud enough. Practice projecting your voice before your presentation. In general, it is better to be too loud than too quiet.

In my teaching experience less than 1% of my students were too loud. Your aim as a presenter is to be heard and understood. People cannot understand you if they cannot hear you.

## Air Intake

It is easier for you to speak loudly and powerfully if you breathe properly. Effective air intake and appropriate pauses during your talk will help you control the volume of your voice. Slow down your delivery if you are having volume difficulty. Breathe from your diaphragm or stomach and not from your chest.

Make yourself "fat" and you will have all the air you need. Practice proper breathing as much as possible before you present.

See daily exercises to help you improve your vocal cords, Page 194 on Preparation.

# Vary Your Voice

Vocal variety is very important when you speak. Periodically change your speed, pitch, and volume going neither too fast nor too slow. Do not mumble in a monotone. A deeper tone signals more confidence than a high pitched one. Also, if you catch yourself stumbling or not knowing what to say, slow down and possibly even stop to catch your breath and collect your thoughts. If you blank out or choke, just smile! Only people with great self-confidence can smile, therefore the audience will assume you know what you are doing!

At the time you rehearse, practice using your voice to emphasize certain words and phrases. You should train your voice to deliver on its own so that your brain can concentrate solely on the message.

When we are nervous we tend to speak faster. Rapid flow of words encourages shallow breathing. If you want to reinforce an image of confidence, slow down. It is much easier for you to breathe deeply when you don't speak too quickly. The audience will also be impressed by the power you project.

# Use Your Voice for Emphasis

Slow down and lower your volume to a near whisper if you want to catch the audience's attention for a point you are making. However, they should still be able to hear you. This change in pitch will signal the listeners that you are about to make a point and they must listen more closely.

You must show a contrast in volume in order for this to work properly. To capture and if necessary, recapture the audience's attention, pause at strategic intervals for a moment. Be silent, take a couple of deep breaths and make eye contact with key members of the audience before proceeding.

Practice these phrases using vocal pauses and decreasing volume:

*"People have made our company profitable."*

*"Never again will we be caught off guard by the dissatisfaction of our customers."*

*"The key to increasing our share of the market is innovation."*

Know how to use vocal inflection to change the meaning and impact of different phrases. Use it in different ways. Remember, it is not only what you say but the way that you say it that counts.

You can say things in a very blunt and direct manner if you use the right inflection and tone of voice. See how many different ways you can say these sentences:

*"You can do it!"*
*"Congratulations, John!"*
Or more negatively, *"You're fired!"*.

Or try these variations:

| | |
|---|---|
| *"**I** didn't tell Susan, Peter is stupid."* | Someone else must have done so. |
| *"I **didn't** tell Susan, Peter is stupid."* | But I soon might. |
| *"I didn't **tell** Susan, Peter is stupid."* | I only hinted it. |
| *"I didn't tell **Susan**, Peter is stupid."* | But I told Jackie. |
| *"I didn't tell Susan, **Peter** is stupid."* | I said John. |
| *"I didn't tell Susan, Peter **is** stupid."* | But he certainly was. |
| *"I didn't tell Susan, Peter is **stupid**."* | Just that he is dumb. |

# If You Have a Foreign Accent

There is no doubt that you will have to try harder to make yourself understood if your first language is not the same as your audience. Accents can make it difficult for others to understand you and that, of course, leads to confusion.

In general, if you have rapport with your listeners and they see you trying hard to do your best, they will be patient and make the extra effort to understand you. Here are some steps which can help your audience grasp your message:

• Start off slowly, then gradually speed up. Lots of well known speakers do this. They begin slowly so that the audience can adjust to their accent, then speed up to their normal rate of speech so everyone can follow right along.

• Sprinkle your presentation with one or two phrases from your native language, then translate them. This will personalize your speech, build rapport, and remind everyone that you are indeed fluent in your mother tongue!

• If you are not comfortable in the language being used, rely on visuals to reinforce your message. Put extra care into the preparation of these materials. Be sure that they all are grammatically correct and written using a vocabulary appropriate for the group. Watch figures of speech and regional expressions. What seems like a proper translation may have funny or offensive connotations that may catch you off guard and embarrass you. This will put you under even more stress, so plan to minimize such occurrences. Ask a friend to proof read your materials and check for errors. If you are not comfortable speaking the language you are to present in, you may want to build your entire speech around visual aids and demonstrations. In this way, your slower than average speed of delivery will be offset by the impact of your visual images. The main thing is to keep the audience's attention. Do not let them become bored.

## How to Improve Your Voice

Be aware of your vocal tone and make adjustments as necessary. Learn to listen to yourself as you talk. Keep in mind that your voice sounds different to you than to others.

Get a small tape recorder. Record your speeches. Pay attention to how you talk on the telephone. Experiment reciting different phrases. Play back the tapes and analyse yourself.

Can you adjust your pitch, vary your volume, add pauses or pace your delivery more appropriately?

You can control your voice more easily when you are conscious of how you sound before you speak. Always practice, practice, practice.

Some people end in a questioning tone when they are nervous.

"Hello, my name is Susan?" (I think it is) (If it is okay with you).

Or they become more authoritative.

"My name is Sylvester". (Get it right or I'll kill you!).

Be aware that your voice changes when you are nervous. Practice deep breathing to help you relax and speak in a normal tone.

# Cliches to Avoid

Here are some definite traps. It's surprising how commonly and freely these are used. Do your audience a favor and eliminate them completely from your speaking style:

*"Unaccustomed as I am to public speaking..."*

Do not worry, it will show soon enough! Do not make excuses or comments about the fact you have never presented before. Everybody does that. Do not say how much you hate to make presentations. Tell them you enjoy presenting and look forward to this occasion.

*"I don't know why I have been asked to speak today..."*

If you don't know, you should sit down and be quiet! Don't waste anyone's time. Never speak if you do not know what to say.

*"I haven't really prepared anything..."*

When presenters start with this, everyone wonders why they are presenting. Do you want to waste their time? I personally think it is terribly rude to begin like that.

*"Speaking off the top of my head..."*

What does that mean? Is it possible to speak from the bottom of your feet? Anyway, your lack of preparation will be obvious to everybody. Do not draw attention to it.

*"You know..."*

This is a typical nervous habit. Listen to your everyday conversations and you will certainly hear it too. Generally, people who say, "you know", want feedback. In public speaking you will have to learn to control this.

*"Uh...Uhhh....Ummmm...."*

The #1 killer of speakers and conversationalists everywhere. Saying nothing is better than "Uhhh". Stop to collect your thoughts first, then talk. What's surprising is that some believe that "Uh..." makes you sound more intelligent and reflective! Nothing could be farther from the truth. Do not mumble during a presentation, ever! Speak English instead. If you cannot remember what to say, shut up and think. The audience will appreciate it if you do.

*"For all intents and purposes..."*

What does that stand for? This is pure babbling and does not have any meaning in itself. Do not say it.

*"So on and so forth...."*

Another empty, useless, unnecessary phrase.

*"Today I am going to speak about..."*

This is an amateurish way of beginning. Sadly, too many start off that way. There is no power in this kind of opening. Grab your audience with something original! Practice your attention-getting first sentence. Write it out exactly as you plan to deliver it.

## Talking on the Way to the Podium

Never, ever do that. This is a clear indication of nervousness. Talking or giggling is an absolute giveaway of the great pressure you are going through.

## How To Ensure a Powerful Opening

Walk slowly and confidently to the lectern. Be sure that all of your visual aids and whatever else you need are set up in advance, so that when you start everything is ready for you to use. Try to avoid arranging your equipment in front of the audience, but if you have to, do not keep them waiting more than necessary.

Once behind the lectern (if you absolutely have to use one), take a deep breath and smile.

Take another breath and begin. The longer you pause before beginning to speak, the more power you gain. By pausing, you are forcing the audience to anticipate you. They will be more attentive. It is important for you to be physically and mentally ready to give a presentation. If you are not ready, do not begin.

# How to End a Speech

As with your opening and, like a flight, your presentation should have a smooth conclusion that neatly ties everything together. I recommend that you do not read your closing statement from notes. Do have it ready in case you have a "brown-out". However, to ensure sincerity, your closing should come from within as much as possible. The delivery, if not the content, should be spontaneous.

Here are a few effective approaches that can be prepared in advance:

## Summarize Your Presentation

Reiterate your objective in speaking and demonstrate that you have fulfilled that purpose. End with things like,

> *"In summary, there are five ways we can keep our customers for ever"*

> or

> *In conclusion, there are three points I want to summarize...".*

## Close With an Anecdote

The story should tie everything together and exemplify the kind of action or behavior you expect from your listener as a result of your presentation.

Use one which effectively illustrates your most important point and makes the audience feel good.

# End with a Call to Action

Tell the audience exactly what you think they should do. This is critical yet so many just assume that the listeners will know what to do. Some speakers feel that a call to action insults the audience's intelligence. On the contrary, the call to action removes any doubt as to what you are trying to communicate to them. Here are some examples:

*"Start today to sincerely compliment your employees if you want to increase productivity in your department"*

*"Phone your local community college today and register for a course in public speaking..."*

*"When you go home, ask your children about their life goals and listen to them without passing judgment".*

Tell the audience exactly what they can do in reaction to your speech. Leave them feeling in control.

# Ask a Rhetorical Question

This is one which does not demand an answer so much as reflection on the part of the audience. A rhetorical question should provoke thought. For example:

*"Where would our company be without our leading management group?"*

*"What would we do if we lost our largest client?"*

*"Where would our company be without our five biggest customers?"*

# Make a Statement

In a technical presentation or possibly a press conference, a simple, straightforward concluding statement is all that is necessary to draw your presentation to a close. For example,

> *"There is much to be learned in this rapidly expanding area of behavioral research into effective employer/employee relations. I've covered just a small part of it. I hope that each of you will take time to learn more..."*

# End the Same Way You Began

This is a popular movie-making technique. It gives symmetry to your presentation. You can close with the same anecdote or quotation with which you opened and show that you have come full circle. For example:

> *"As I quoted from F.D.R. at the beginning of my presentation, 'We have nothing to fear but fear itself'..."*

> *"I would like to end where I began. Our customers are Number One. Without them, we would not exist..."*

# Show them an Outline of Your Completed Presentation

Similar to the above "bookends" approach, this technique neatly and concisely summarizes everything you have tried to cover and smoothly leads the way to questions from the audience.

## "In closing my presentation..."

This regains the attention of the listeners and sets you up to make a summary statement or call to action. Although it may sound amateurish it is a good way to keep the audience awake on a "sleeper" topic.

## "I want to leave you with..."

Using this technique, you are giving your listeners something more: an idea, a piece of advice. Make it useful and be sure that it leaves them feeling good.

Above all, when you conclude your presentation, smile with all of your pride - stand tall. Walk slowly to your seat and look as confident as you can. Even if you screwed up, you are probably the only one who noticed! But when you have finished, everyone will watch you again and judge you by the way you returned confidently to your seat. So, keep your shoulders back, your chin up and smile!

My principal message in this book is that communicating to a business audience is much more than simply giving a speech. You must present yourself and your ideas in total. This is one of the secrets to power presentations.

# Summary
# Secrets to Delivering
# A Powerful Speech

- Fit your topic to your audience's interests. Communicate in their language.

- Organize your presentation. Know your main points well.

- Never read your speech from a text. Use minimal notes.

- Practice and rehearse your speech over and over. Preferably in front of real people. Otherwise on your feet.

- Dramatize, emphasize, energize.

- Pause frequently.

- Tell them you are looking forward to your presentation.

- Start up slowly and then gradually speed up to a comfortable pace.

- Look happy and confident. Smile.

*The heart of a fool
is in his mouth,
but the mouth of a wise man
is in his heart.*

*— Benjamin Franklin*

BODY LANGUAGE – Equipment – Environment – Preparation – Speech –

*Give me beauty
in the inward soul;
may the outward
and the
inward man be
as one.*

*— Socrates*

# THE SECOND ESSENTIAL:

# BODY LANGUAGE

**R**esearch in communication has consistently shown that messages are conveyed in many ways besides words. Dr. Albert Mehrabian stated in his book "Silent Messages" that the believability of what we communicate is influenced 7% by words, 38% by tone of voice and 55% by body language. In other words, 93% of the message is conveyed using "paralanguage".

Our bodies speak volumes. We are always sending signals to others whether we like it or not. Body language, combined with vocal tone, can override or even cancel the meaning of the words you say. Therefore, it is important to ensure your body and your mouth are in concurrence and sending the same signal! It is also of great significance for you to control your non-verbal messages as much as your verbal ones.

## Analyse Yourself

Look in a mirror and make typical gestures and facial expressions (close the door so no one sees you doing it). Ask a friend to analyse you as you perform various expressions. The best way to become aware of your body language is to videotape yourself speaking in front of a group. If you do not have an opportunity to do that, record yourself in rehearsal. This will give a true picture of the way others see you. After watching yourself, you will know what adjustments are necessary.

We're all human. We're all somewhat self-conscious when it comes to seeing ourselves. Yet, a lot of our communication power comes not from what we say, but how we say it. It is, therefore, important that we use body language to our greatest advantage. Self analysis will help us to improve dramatically. Self observation will show which gestures look natural and which ones do not. Trust yourself. Work on conveying emotion through physical expression. Learn to show natural enthusiasm, confidence, anger, concern and sympathy.

## Facial Expressions

While 55% of the message is transmitted by your body, most of this is communicated by your head – specifically, through your eyes, eyebrows and mouth.

Facial expressions can make a world of difference. Think of the last time someone told you they were not upset and you didn't believe them.

Our moods and feelings are easily observed through our body signals. The impact of your gestures and facial statements is immense. Learn to use them more. But, be careful that they appear natural to your listeners.

Abraham Lincoln once said that, by the age of forty a person is totally responsible for the look on their face. At first, that sounded strange to me. Abe himself didn't look terribly handsome. But he was right. Years of worrying and unhappiness result in wrinkles. The muscles on your face will get used to frowning if you do not exercise them by smiling. Your eyes will slowly shrink if you do not brighten them up with positive thoughts.

The combination of your mouth, eyes and eyebrows can result in an infinite variety of expressions to go with your words. Practice in front of a mirror or videotape repeating the same phrases with different expressions and pronunciations.

For example, try "When the going gets tough, the tough get going!" Change your facial expressions with practice. Refine and integrate them into your next presentation.

# Smile

Studies have shown that people who smile are happier than those who do not. Sounds logical. In 1872, Charles Darwin actually published a treatise on emotion and facial expressions.

Today many scientists have proven that smiling releases a chemical in your brain that makes you feel good. However, you can only smile if you feel confident, comfortable and in control.

Job applicants who smile during their interviews are more likely to be hired. We tend to want to avoid people who frown all the time. Who wants to spend time with a grouch?

It has been shown that kids in school get more attention from the teacher and therefore could obtain better grades if they smile.

Bank managers are more likely to lend you money if you softly smile when they ask you all those questions.

Smiling during a presentation is therefore very important. Subconsciously, your audience will feel better about themselves and they'll also think you know what you are doing. Your positive attitude will rub off.

Keep smiling and soon they'll be smiling too. A sincere, gentle smile is also a great way to establish rapport with listeners at the beginning. Try it!

Depending on the subject of your presentation it's not always appropriate to wear a grin. If you have to fire someone or give a eulogy at a funeral, I do not suggest that you put on a happy face.

Just because your topic is serious doesn't mean you need to look bored. Show a happy face to add contrast to your presentation. Smile at positive points and then switch to a sober expression at critical points. This contrast, if natural, will add emphasis to your ideas.

## The Value of a Smile

*It costs nothing, but creates much.*
*It enriches those who receive,*
*without impoverishing those who give.*
*It happens in a flash and the memory*
*of it sometimes lasts forever.*
*None are so rich that they can get along*
*without it and none are so poor but are*
*richer for its benefits.*
*It creates happiness in the home, fosters*
*goodwill in a business and is the*
*countersign of friends.*
*It is rest to the weary, daylight to the*
*discouraged, sunshine to the sad and*
*nature's best antidote for trouble.*
*Yet it cannot be bought, borrowed, begged*
*or stolen, for it is something that is*
*no earthly good to anybody 'til it is given away.*

*— Unknown*

# Eye Contact

Effective and efficient eye contact is the mark of a professional presenter. According to Leonardo da Vinci, the eyes are the mirror of the soul. They show how you feel inside. Open eyes convey belief in oneself. Eyes half-closed signal disbelief. Good eye contact helps you to carry your message individually to each person in the audience. Learn to scan the audience, stopping to make eye contact with each individual in the room. Pause two or three seconds with each listener. This ensures that your presentation feels more like a one-on-one conversation than a speech.

Looking people straight in the eyes builds trust. If you are not comfortable doing that, look at the bridge of the nose or at the chin. The effect is exactly the same and it appears to others as if you are looking at them directly. Scan the room diagonally. From corner to corner. Left to right, right to left. If there is someone in the audience whom you think might intimidate you or cause you to lose confidence, avoid looking at them until you are comfortable and your presentation well underway. It is important to use techniques which reinforce your confidence and help build rapport with your audience. Look for the friendlier, sympathetic faces. Smile at these people and win them over, one by one. Then, move on to the more sceptical members and work on them. Your audience will tend to look at you the way you look at them. If you smile they will smile. If you frown, so will they.

## Visualize the Audience Looking Silly

If you are nervous making eye contact with the audience, and most presenters are at the beginning, just use your imagination to picture the audience sitting nude – especially if they're all big shots! At the beginning of his career, Winston Churchill imagined the members of his audiences sitting in their underwear! Or imagine that they all owe you money...a *lot* of money!

# Gestures

Learn to speak with your hands. Use them to point at imaginary objects and draw lines in the air in front of you (in general, pointing at others is not a polite gesture). Never aim at specific members in the audience with your index finger. If you must point your finger, direct away from the group toward an imaginary enemy or competitor. Unlocked hands help convey openness and honesty. Size or quantity can be shown by expanding or contracting the space between your hands.

When delineating the main ideas of your presentation, count them out on your fingers as you go. For example, "point number three (hold out three fingers) involves the relations between the company and its employees...". Anytime you refer to figures of less than ten, you can gracefully show your audience the appropriate number of fingers. Hold your hands at a 45 degree angle from your head and gesture high enough so that everyone can see them.

To emphasize physical size such as length or width, hold your hands out in front of you widely apart and move them up and down. To stress the narrowness of something, position your hands or thumb and index finger vertically about two inches apart in front of you.

Make sure your gestures are smooth and natural. Do not use too many or deliver them too mechanically. Study the television evangelists and note the ones who over-gesture. Work on appearing sincere and comfortable with yourself.

## Keep Your Hands Out of Your Pockets

If you have difficulty shaking this habit, clip your pockets closed with safety pins. But never put your hands in your pockets. It implies that you are unsure or conversely, too comfortable. Also, remove coins, keys or other jingling or bulky items from your pants. This will prevent you from making distracting clinking noises. You will also look better.

Another good idea is to get rid of all pens and other items from your shirt and jacket pockets. These objects could distract your audience. It also prevents you from fiddling with your eyeglasses, pens, coins or keys if they are hidden in your briefcase.

Do not hold your hands behind your back for too long. Have them visible and keep them comfortable. Move them as your body moves. If they are not visible, your body appears too stiff. If you don't know what to do with your hands, before or during a presentation, try the following:

## Where To Put Your Hands

- **Let your hands and arms drop naturally to your side.**

- **Gently fold your index fingers together without wringing or gripping the hands in anyway.**

- **Start your presentation and let your hands do what they want to do, – as long as they do not want to go into your pockets or make obscene gestures to your listeners!**

## Shoulders

Your shoulders can help convey confidence. In contrast, they can also make you appear tense and nervous. If you position them to the back, you will actually feel more self-assured. If you have them pulled back, tilt your head slightly upwards and you'll have all the poise to take on the largest audience!

Imagine feeling depressed as you push your shoulders straight back and hold your head up. It doesn't work! To make yourself feel sad, unhappy and sluggish, you must drop your shoulders and tilt your head down.

Your body posture effects your emotions and how you feel determines your posture. They influence one another. If you are confident, happy, and ready, your body will show it.

# Shoulders and Head Positioning

| Confident and Positive | Nervous and Negative |
|:---:|:---:|
|  |  |
| Shoulders back | Shoulders drooping |
| Head up | Head down |
| Smile | Frown |
| Full of energy | Low energy |
| Ready to perform | Not ready |
| I am great! | I'm no good! |
| Yes I can! | No I cannot! |
|  |  |
| Life is great! | Life is rotten! |

# Movement

How your body moves (or doesn't move) is extremely important to communication. A speaker who stays in one place could become boring. Lack of movement restrains your emotions. Don't hesitate to vary your position; shifting toward and away from your audience and from side to side can help emphasize your points.

It will keep listeners interested in what you are saying – provided it doesn't distract them. Decide how much variety of movement is appropriate. Experiment. Walk so the audience will be able to see your body better as well as hear you more clearly.

If you are in a board room, walk around the table so that everyone is able to see you. Regular, physical movement is good for your breathing and circulation. It builds your energy level and helps keep you relaxed and feeling more confident in front of the group.

# What If You Drop Something?

If something should fall to the floor during a presentation – such as a pen or a piece of paper – watch your speed and posture as you pick it up. Subconsciously, the audience will judge you by how you move.

If you stoop down very quickly to pick up the object, the audience may think you are nervous. Instead, pick it up slowly and gracefully. Older folks do it that way all the time!

We often think that older people have more self-assurance but age alone has nothing to do with having more confidence.

When I gave regular university courses in public speaking, I was amazed at the variety of students enrolled – lawyers, police officers, doctors, accountants, nurses, – old ones, young ones. The more mature students were not always more self-assured. When you are older you just *look* and *act* more confident.

If you are getting on in years and you drop something, argh! – it just takes you a while to bend down and straighten up again. But others subconsciously think, "Hey, they are very confident". The moral: Go slower when you present and your listeners will think that you are more self-assured in what you are doing.

## *The Spirit of Youth*

*Youth is not a time of life; it is a state of mind. Nobody grows old by living a number of years. People grow old only by deserting their ideals.*

*Years wrinkle the skin; but to give up enthusiasm wrinkles the soul.*

*Worry, doubt, self distrust, fear and despair - these are the long, long years that bow the heart and turn the greening spirit back to dust.*

*You are as young as your faith; as old as your doubt; as young as your self-confidence; as old as your fear; as young as your hope; as old as your despair.*

*— Unknown*

## Stand Up

You may find yourself reluctant to stand if you are at a conference table and all the presenters before you spoke while seated. Yet, it is always better to speak on your feet. Here is a useful trick: Plant something in your briefcase on the other side of the room and use that as an excuse to rise and walk around to retrieve it.

Another excuse is to rise and distribute your handout materials to each person in the room. Then, just remain standing. This position will help you breathe more deeply and project your voice more easily.

You will also look taller. Subconsciously, we listen more when looking up than when looking down.

*Do the thing you fear to do*
*and keep on doing it . . .*
*that is the quickest and surest*
*way ever yet discovered*
*to conquer fear.*

*— Dale Carnegie*

# How You Stand is Everything

- Tilt your head slightly upward

- Stick your chin out

- Drain the air from your cheeks. Exhale

- Smile softly

- Let your eyes shine, sparkling and clear

- Move your eyes slowly, but surely and look at each participant as you go around the room

- Stand with your shoulders back

- Keep your chest out and stomach in

- Hold your hands open, relaxed. Do not stick them in your pockets

- Have your knees relaxed and not locked

- Your spine should be straight – Do not slouch!

- Stand with your feet slightly apart, <u>both</u> men and women!

- Breathe slowly, deeply, and evenly

# Analyse the Physical Style of Your Audience

All people have different physical characteristics. Body language is actually a very complicated science. There are many books on the subject which can provide insight into the non-verbal messages you convey. However, you can learn a lot from your own observations of folks you meet every day. Study patterns in your audiences. With practice you will become skilled at identifying important non-verbal messages.

One of the secrets of better communication is using body language to mirror your audience. Tailor your movements and gestures to match theirs. When beginning your presentation, start off slowly and adjust your speed to suit the group. Go slowly until you have had a chance to study the style and mood of your listeners. Bankers, doctors, accountants and engineers may be serious and want you to go slowly. Sales and marketing people and younger audiences may want speed, animation, and action. Keep in mind, one of the best kept secrets of building rapport: be just a bit more enthusiastic than your audience!

Not all human beings communicate in the same way. Essentially there are two kinds of people: those whose primary mode of communication is verbal (listeners) and those whose dominant mode is visual (readers). Verbal people prefer to talk and hear. They think in terms of sounds. Visual people emphasize images and are generally quite interested in complicated visual details. Determine the dominating type in your audience and adjust your communication approach accordingly. At the end of your presentation suggest a particular book that your audience can read. The "visuals" will love you for doing this.

> *The most successful politician is he who says what everybody is thinking most often and in the loudest voice*
>
> — *Theodore Roosevelt*

| Listeners (Verbal) | Readers (Visual) |
|---|---|
|  |  |
| *How To Observe:* | *How To Observe:* |
| **Loud audience**<br>**Very excited**<br>**More smiles**<br>**Outgoing**<br>**Responsive** | **Quiet audience**<br>**Critical looking**<br>**Serious expressions**<br>**Introverted**<br>**Passive** |
|  |  |
| *How To Handle Them:* | *How To Handle Them:* |
| **Demonstrate**<br>**Dramatize**<br>**Jump up and down**<br>**Go faster**<br>**Not too many details**<br><br>**Use hand gestures**<br><br>**Entertain** | **Theorize**<br>**Do not dramatize**<br>**Stand still**<br>**Slow down**<br>**Give them lots of information**<br>**Keep hands close to your body**<br>**Inform with fact** |

## Handling Nervousness

Even though you speak often in front of many audiences, there will still be times when you feel uptight – that is a fact of life. It's important for you to be able to control your nervousness. You might give a toast at a corporate function or possibly a wedding. You pick up your glass of champagne in view of everyone and suddenly your hand starts to shake violently. However, you know you must hold the goblet until you finish the toast. If this happens, there are three things you can do. One is to quickly drink the contents of your glass (this is *definitely* not recommended!). The second is to postpone your announcement until you feel more comfortable (this is not very practical as you cannot keep them waiting forever). The third is to bring the glass close to your chest so that it rests against your body. The audience will not even notice and you will be able to concentrate on giving a good toast. Toward the end of the speech you can shift it gracefully away, holding it perfectly still in mid-air in front of you.

In general, if your hands start to shake, just move them temporarily out of view. Hold them very briefly behind your back or rest them at your sides. Never put them in your pockets! The audience will watch what you do with them. If you move them slowly, smoothly and gracefully, you will look confident.

*In great attempts
it is glorious even to fail*

*— Vince Lombardi*

118

# Typical Signs of Nervousness

- Hands in pockets
- Increased blinking of the eyes
- Failure to make eye contact
- Looking at the floor
- Shaking legs
- Licking and biting of the lips
- Clenching teeth
- Finger tapping
- Jittery hands
- Fist clenching
- Faster, jerkier gestures
- Sweaty hands and armpits
- Cracking voice
- Increased rate of speech
- Clearing of the throat
- Pulling at skin
- Frequent smoothing of hair
- Standing on sides of feet rather than flat on floor
- Toes wiggling
- Buttocks clamped tightly together

# HOW TO DRESS – or –
# "KLEIDER MACHEN LEUTE"

This old Swiss saying is very true, clothes do make the person. The way you dress has a lot to do with what the audience thinks of you. If you wear the "right" clothes they will assume that you are successful. If you appear in casual dress, they will think that you are a casual person. And so on.

An experiment was conducted in which an actor, dressed as a business executive in a dark suit and carrying an expensive attache case, stood on a street corner of a large city and proceeded to ask for money. He gave the story that he had forgotten his wallet at home as he approached passersby for bus fare. Other businessmen stopped to talk to him and many offered him several dollars, some suggesting that he take a cab. At the end of the day, the actor had made several hundred dollars.

The next day of the experiment, the actor dressed only in casual jeans and a windbreaker. He stood on the same busy street corner and asked for change to make a telephone call, saying that he wanted to apply for a job that he saw advertised in a newspaper. This time the response was different. As the man asked passersby, people would pause in hesitation. They wondered what he would really do with the quarter. They questioned his sincerity. At the end of the day, he had made less than twenty dollars.

Finally, on the third day of the experiment, the actor put on his worst clothes and dressed like a bum. On the same busy corner, he stuck out his hat and asked for change and nearly everyone ignored him. Only a few people stopped at all.

What happened? It was the same man, in three different disguises and there were three different results. The experiment showed that perception is reality. People are more likely to spend time to help an apparently prosperous individual than someone who looks down and out. Thus, the moral of the story is that the way you look and dress determines how the audience will react to your presentation – whether on the street or in a board room.

## How to Dress For a Power Presentation

Here are a few basic ideas to follow:

– Know the style of your audience. While it is okay to be different, be sure you do not stand out too much (at least until you have proven yourself!). Once everyone knows what a genius you are, clothe yourself in any garments you chose. But get your priorities straight. When meeting a new group and the first impression is crucial, dress in the same fashion as your audience. Whether it's dark suits or sport jackets, formal womens' dresses or pants, try to match.

– Aim to look just slightly more conservative than your audience. Wear clothes similar to the better dressed members of the audience. Remember, you are trying to establish rapport and trust. A conservative style will cause them to take you more seriously. Flashiness arouses suspicion. Once you have won over the audience and, if you are presenting over a period of time, you can ease up a bit. But maintain a look of professionalism. Wear colors and patterns that complement each other – like dark blue and red. Do not over do it. Be creative but use common sense.

– Always appear as neat and clean as possible. Choose colors that withstand wear and fabrics which do not wrinkle. If necessary, wear something over your clothes (particularly when eating) to protect them and keep them clean until you make your presentation.

– Dress the way you want to be perceived. If you want to be seen as a top executive, dress like one. By looking the part you are psychologically reinforcing that goal for yourself and others around you. Your boss might start to see you in a more challenging role if you appear to be in command.

– Look trim. If you are, this is half the battle. Clothes tend to drape better on slim people. If you aren't slender ...well, you might consider reducing. Meanwhile, it is especially important to choose clothing carefully with an eye to the colors, fabric and style which streamline your appearance. Be sure that clothing fits properly; you will neither feel comfortable in a too snug outfit, nor will you look good.

Become aware of your image and dress to balance it. For example, a petite woman executive might wish to avoid feminine, flowery dresses for business. Her corporate credibility may be enhanced if she chooses simple outfits in rich, powerful colors.

Conversely, women who have developed a "severe, no nonsense" image in the corporate world, may wish to soften their appearance by the deliberate use of "feminine" fabrics and accessories.

Appearing too young, believe it or not, can also be a problem. Men and women who wish to project a more mature image should choose darker "power" colors.

– If I had only one suit or dress, it would be dark blue. It is the number one color for presentations as it reinforces the audience's trust in the speaker. It looks professional, successful, timeless and reassuring!

– For shirts and blouses, white is always the best choice. It implies purity and trustworthiness. Light blue or beige are also acceptable. Stripes and patterns might be too flashy, and of course, change with fashion.

– For shoes, again, dark is best. Dark colors, say some experts, show a "down to earth" character. Brown shoes are harder to match and do not go well with anything other than brown outfits. Avoid white, grey or suede shoes.

– Do not appear too fashion conscious. This could imply that you are governed by what others think and are less independent. Fashions tend to change very often. You'll spend a lot of money trying to keep up. Traditional, classic clothing is a better investment and there are still many ways to appear creative.

– For suit jackets, begin your presentation with the buttons closed. Then once you are underway, undo them slowly. This small gesture symbolizes your openness to the audience. It suggests that you are ready for responsive communication.

– Be careful about jewelry, accessories, pens, etc. Make sure these do not distract the audience. As mentioned previously, remove all unnecessary items from your pockets. Avoid bulges caused by keys, wallets, calculators, or dictaphones. Leave these in your attaché case or nearby purse.

– Perfume may enhance your presentation if it is used sparingly and the scent is of good quality. A group of 10 to 20 will certainly notice your choice. If your favorite fragrance builds confidence – by all means use it.

– Above all, dress comfortably and be proud of who you are. Your style of dress as you present should signal, most importantly, that you care about what you are doing. The way you feel is the way you are. Be sure that you look the way you want to be, that is, assured, confident, certain, secure and prepared!

– Briefcases: the thinner they are the more important is your position in the company. (That is what everyone thinks – it does not have to be true!) The darker the color, the more powerful the content. Avoid shiny or wild colored briefcases. Carry in it only the presenting material. *NOTHING ELSE!* Absolutely nothing else.

– Pens should never be seen protruding from jackets or shirt pockets. Please never use a plastic pen in front of a group! I have a lot of them at my office and at home. But be sure not to use them in front of prospective clients or when giving an important presentation.

Cross pens are a good investment; the Montblanc is a far better writing instrument, but more costly. Any black, matte finished imitation is acceptable.

– Eye glasses give the presenter a more intelligent, studious appearance. But, if you don't need to wear them, do not buy any! If you want to make an important statement or would like to be more intimate with your listener, take your glasses off.

–You don't need to buy a Swiss Rolex watch to look powerful. But don't appear with a $6.99 digital either. If you carry the one you inherited from your grandfather, be sure it has a clean, new band. As a rule of thumb, the simpler the dial, the thinner the watch, the more powerful the look.

> *Dress powerful. . .*
> *Stand powerful. . .*
> *But mainly*
> *Think and feel powerful!*
>
> *– Peter Urs Bender*

# Secrets of POWER Looks

- Visit an image consultant for advice on wardrobe planning

- Wear dark colored suits or dresses

- Plain white shirts or blouses

- Red ties or scarves

- Black shoes, freshly polished, (Brogues for men and conservative styles in general)

- Very little jewelry – worn discreetly

- Big earrings for women

- Black Cross pen

- Calm, slow gestures and movements

- Shoulders back, chin up

- Smile briefly, and then put on your POWER look

# Summary
# Secrets To Improve
# Your Body Language

- Love your body. If you are a bit over-weight, adore your figure anyway.

- Stand and sit to your tallest.
  Never slouch.

- If you are unsure of your appearance, check yourself in a mirror before meeting the group.

- Always wear your best clothes.

- Move slowly, deliberately, and gracefully.

- Never rush in front of your audience.

- Shoulders back. Chest out.
  Chin up. Smile!

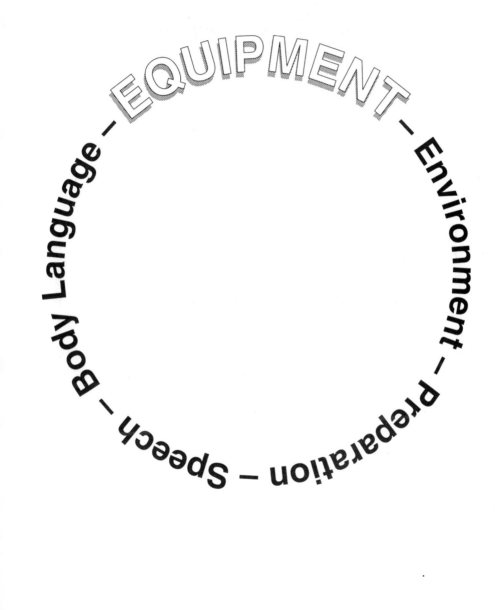

*All the world's a stage,
And all the men and women
merely players.
They have their exits and
their entrances;
And one man in his time
plays many parts.*

*— William Shakespeare*

# THE THIRD ESSENTIAL:

# EQUIPMENT

An old Chinese proverb says that *a picture is worth a thousand words,* so, a demonstration is worth a book. Your presentation is not just words and sounds, but also images, movement and physical interaction with your audience. There are many ways to achieve effective communication with the aid of the right external tools. Your audience will retain more of your message if you use visuals and gadgets to reinforce what you say.

## Lecterns, Podiums, etc.

Most of us get the words "lectern", "podium", "rostrum", and "dais" confused. A lectern is the slanted-top desk you can use when reading your notes during your presentation. It can be placed in the middle or the end of the head table.

A podium is a raised platform on which a speaker stands during a presentation. You will want to use one especially if you are short or there are more than three rows of chairs, so as to ensure everyone in the back of the room can see you. Standing on a platform will also dramatically increase your vocal projection.

A rostrum or dais is a larger platform or stage on which a head table might be placed during a formal dinner.

## Lecterns

It is helpful to have a spot on which to put your notes. The problem is that most speakers hide behind lecterns, thereby greatly constraining important body language. (Refer to page 67) I strongly encourage you not to use them, just as I urge you to use as few notes as possible. Notes are essential only when you must read a prepared speech, or give a presentation in a foreign language. In that case, a lectern with a light and microphone will help you get through your talk smoothly.

However, lecterns do make things look official. The seriousness of your topic, the occasion, and the degree of formality in the audience may require that you use one. If so, plan to start and end behind it, but deliver most of your presentation away from the lectern with your whole body in full view.

There is one important rule about lecterns: Do not keep your hands gripped on the sides! This draws listeners' attention to your nervousness and restrains your body language. However, gripping the sides of the lectern can be a very effective technique for adding emphasis. Appropriately grasp the lectern only once or twice and lean toward the audience to make your critical points. The contrast helps emphasize what you are saying. Practice speaking comfortably without a lectern. If one is available, use it to hold your notes but do not hide behind it as you deliver your talk or you will reduce the power of your presentation.

## Music Stands

While I strongly discourage the use of lecterns, you might want to consider using a wire music stand for your notes. Most hotels have one – you just have to ask. The difference is that they are less obtrusive and small enough that you won't be tempted to rest your hands. Your listeners will clearly be able to see you. If you present from notes or a workbook, you can rest these on the stand. You then have both: all your notes in front of you, plus 100% use of your body to communicate freely and naturally to your audience.

# Microphones

It is essential that your listeners hear you properly. If you speak to a very large group, you need a microphone. Unfortunately, people create all kinds of excuses for not using one. They act as if they had been bitten by one, long ago.

It is important to rehearse in advance so you can feel comfortable working with your microphone. Practice turning it on and off! Sounds simple, but it is the most common problem! Presenters frequently cry: "The sound system does not work".

But they didn't turn on the mike! Always set it to the appropriate height before you begin – two to five inches away from your lips. If you must adjust it while speaking, turn the switch off first, move the stand, then turn it on again. This way, you will not make annoying loud noises. Try to know the name of the person who will operate the sound system and where to adjust the volume on the amplifier. To be on the safe side, have someone in the audience who can turn down the volume if there is feedback.

Feedback is a typical problem with microphones. It's usually caused by one of the following:

– The presenter stands too close to the microphone.

– There is another microphone or certain electronic gadgets close by.

– Hand held microphones are used too close to the sound system's speakers (particularly if they are overhead). This causes a "loop" whereby the sound of your voice coming from the speakers is picked up by the microphone and re-amplified. This can be corrected by walking away from the sound system speakers. If you cannot spot them keep moving until the problem is resolved.

As for your own microphone technique, practice certain phrases to get the right distance. Consonants in particular require some rehearsal, for if you are too close they will make a loud "popping" sound. For example, rehearse words with the letters "P" or "S". Try saying these phrases into your microphone:

*"Perfect prior preparation prevents poor performance"*
*"Peter, Peter pumpkin planter"*
*"Seven successive deficits"*
*"Tremendous titans with terrific temerity"*
*"White walruses wait restlessly for wandering revolutionary riots"*
*"Take care to kindly correct all occurrences of careless criticism"*

If you are speaking outdoors in a stadium of several hundred people, you may have problems with the reverberation of the amplified sound of your voice. (Reverberation is sort of an extra loud echo). Concentrate on listening to your own voice rather than that coming out of the speakers, otherwise, the few split seconds of delay will drive you bananas.

Occasionally, things go wrong with microphones. Often this is because they weren't properly tested and adjusted in advance. For such occasions, it's useful to arm yourself with a few one-liners to ease audience tension (and your own)! Try these one-liners:

•*"I didn't know that it was microphone mating season"*
•*"The more mixed up things get, the more confident I become"*
•*"I prepared for everything, but not for that!"*
•*"Now I lost my place...let's start from the beginning again"*

## Types of Microphones

- **Laveliere**
  It's like a string around your neck
- **Clip-on**
  As you see on TV, clips on your lapel
- **Floor**
  Adjust to your height before using
- **Table**
  Often on discussion panels (Turn it on!)
- **Hand Held**
  Learn to shift it from hand to hand

## Visuals

Because non-verbal signals are so influential in communication, visual aids become important tools that should be used in a presentation. Research into the impact of visuals on memory retention shows that they are very effective in reinforcing what you say:

| | Retention | |
|---|---|---|
| | **After 3 Hours** | **After 3 Days** |
| **Tell Only** | 70% | 10% |
| **Show Only** | 72% | 20% |
| **Show and Tell** | 85% | 65% |

# How We Learn

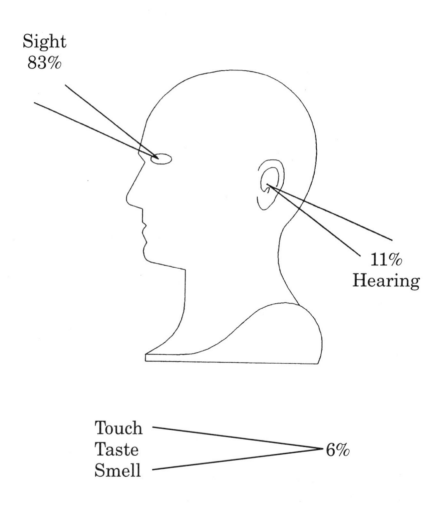

Sight
83%

11%
Hearing

Touch
Taste
Smell

6%

# Visuals In Your Presentation:

- Communicate ideas faster than the spoken word

- Arouse and hold the interest of the audience

- Can explain complicated ideas more easily

- Make you look more organized

- Are especially appropriate for formal meetings

- Re-inforce and enhance your spoken words and increase the probability that all of your message will be understood

- Can be fun. They can add variety to an otherwise dry or serious presentation

- Can be temporary or permanent; dynamic or fixed

- Take some pressure off the presenter by diverting the audience's attention

- Cut across language barriers. This is important for an international or multicultural audience

- Help to clarify different opinions and viewpoints in a controversial subject area

- Make your presentation look more professional

- Provide you with key notes which can be relied on to trigger your memory

- Can be used, over and over, thereby saving you future preparation time

# Special Hints for
# Powerful Presentation Visuals

Focus on presenting only one idea per visual. Choose your words carefully. The fewer, the better. Large advertising billboards have only about five words in total for maximum impact! Avoid clutter. It is easier to read short bullet points than long lines of text. Separate each point with a number and an underlined title.

Above all, make sure that your visuals actually do have a message. Do **not** show pictures, pie charts, or tables of numbers unless they are essential to the point being made. Again, less is more. If it doesn't add anything, leave it out, no matter how impressive you think it looks.

If you have favorite quotations, cartoons, or statistical charts, prepare an attractive transparency or slide. Use colors to keep the audience's attention.

## Explain the Visual

Maintain eye contact with your listeners. Do not talk to the overhead screen or your flipchart! Never, ever speak with your back to the audience (even if they think you look better from behind).

Particularly if you are presenting to a large group, read the visual aid out loud to ensure that everyone sees it. Audience members with vision problems appreciate this. Don't always assume everyone can easily read what you show them.

## Computers

Data presented with the help of a computer can look very impressive. However, you are still the presenter – not the computer. Remember, Murphy might visit you ...

Today there are sophisticated software packages and laser printers for use in preparing powerful presentation visuals. However, do not buy your software the night before your presentations.

If you have a PC or a Macintosh, why not invest in a graphics package? In no time you can create very effective charts, graphs and diagrams.

Computer generated slide kits are easily available and are very useful when you want to tailor your presentation with up-to-the-minute ideas. Presenters working with fluctuating data appreciate being able to make last minute corrections to visuals.

## Instant Slides

Polaroid is one company that makes a variety of visual imaging equipment. Instant films can save a lot of time if you want to develop tailored visuals. Why not show some appropriate slides of group members and weave them into your talk? Everyone will appreciate the personalized touch offered and most are pleased to see their image on a big screen!

## Handouts

Photocopied or printed pages are the most basic visual aid. They provide an easy back-up to your verbal message. They can convey pictures, tables, charts, lists, diagrams, quizzes, forms, and graphs. Typically, they are used to provide summary notes of your talk. The value of handouts is that they are permanent. The audience will have them long after you have given your presentation and hopefully they will be reviewed by them in future.

Because handouts last long after you finish your presentation, they must have a very polished look. Unlike the words you utter, a mistake made in print is there for life! Be sure the typing is neat and that your grammar and spelling is flawless.

Space the type neatly for easy reading. Be certain that the copies are clean and clear. Have a first class print shop do them to be on the safe side. Use colored paper so that your handouts stand out and look different.

## When to Distribute Your Handouts

If you can avoid it, do not present any printed material before you begin your presentation, unless you absolutely must have your audience read along as you speak. Handouts can distract the listeners from paying attention to you.

Explain your ideas first, then the printed material later to reinforce your message. You may want to show the material on an overhead transparency or slide, then pass the handout at the end of your presentation. Be sure to tell the audience that they will receive a copy later.

However, there is no rule of thumb for handouts. You might want to give the audience a printed outline of your main points at the beginning so they can follow along. Other times you will want to present your points orally and visually and provide a detailed, printed summary at the end.

Please remember: handouts can distract the audience so use them with care. If you distribute them during your presentation, do it quickly and efficiently. Organize your pages in advance. When giving them out, pass several piles at once from different points in the room.

When you distribute your handouts, always say, "I hope I have enough". This dramatically increases the perceived value of the material. Everyone will want a copy if there seems to be a shortage. Tell your audience what they should retain from your handouts. Help them focus on the most important information.

# Presentation Workbooks

If your handout contains many pages or if it is likely to be well used, you might consider putting the sheets together with a plastic binding. Use a specially printed cover with the company or organization logo to customize the material.

Handout booklets create a very professional impression. They also help ensure that you do not forget anything! The disadvantage is that the audience may become distracted by flipping ahead in the book to see what's next. Tell them this is forbidden and threaten them with a penalty! An advantage though, and one not to be overlooked, is that the participants will be more likely to save your handouts after the presentation if they are neatly packaged. It will also be easier for them to review your whole proposal at a later date.

# Encourage Notetaking

One of the essential ingredients for learning is spaced repetition. As often as you can, encourage your audience to take notes during your presentation. If you want your group to retain the material, encourage them to review their notes often. Your presentation will then be more likely to have a lasting impact. Key words and simple illustrations will help your participants retain your message. Ask them in advance to take note of what you will say and they will listen more attentively. Encourage them to mark, underline and circle key words on your handouts.

In my own "Presentation" seminar each participant receives a workbook. There are only 8-10 key words printed per page. With each audience I strongly urge them to circle, underline or even cross out the points! They have the right to be wrong!

## Proofread Your Material

Check and re-check any handouts or visuals using numbers to ensure accuracy.

As with spelling, there will always be someone in your audience who will catch mistakes in your material! Do your utmost to eliminate this by having someone, preferably smarter than you, go over the material in advance. It is hard to proofread what you have written yourself.

This advice applies to all pre-printed material: handouts, overheads, slides, flipcharts, etc. Advance preparation minimizes problems and embarrassments. Get someone to help you.

# Handouts

| Type | When to Give Out |
| --- | --- |
| Plain note paper | Before starting presentation |
| Key words only | At start of presentation |
| Diagrams, quotes, quizzes | During or toward end |
| Brochures, order forms | Toward end of presentation |
| Fully-detailed notes | After presentation |
| References and readings | After presentation |

# Models

A very effective way to demonstrate your point is to use three dimensional models or samples. They are particularly useful in product introduction sessions where the audience is actually shown the new item during the presentation. They provide visual stimulation for your audience. Be sure that they are large enough to be seen. If they are too big they should be reduced in size. If too small, be sure to enlarge them.

Place your models and samples in a central spot in the meeting room, so that everyone will be able to see as you demonstrate. If this isn't possible, position the samples so that they can be easily viewed at the conclusion of your presentation. We all like to be shown something. However, it's not a good idea to pass your model around in the audience during your session as this distracts group attention from you.

Be careful, as well, when passing around expensive samples like gold coins, gadgets or expensive art objects – you may not get them back! Instead, invite the listeners to take a look at the end of your show.

Do not use models for the sake of using them. Always have a purpose. When in doubt, do not use any. It is better to have too few models than too many. But one is always better than none!

Make notes that refer to your models and mount them directly on the back of each object. In this way, you can hold them up for the viewer's benefit while reading the technical information on the back! No one will notice that you are looking at notes and everyone will be very impressed that you gave such a detailed explanation from memory.

# Pictures and Drawings

If you use drawings, be sure that people understand what you show them. Tell them what they are looking at! There is nothing worse than to reveal a drawing and have everybody wonder what it is. Be sure that the work is large enough for the entire audience to see. Otherwise, put it in handouts and distribute it at the end of your presentation.

# Graphs

If you refer to statistics, talk about trends, or compare percentages, use a bar or pie chart. It's much easier for your audience to understand the difference between 67% and 33% if they can visualize it. Bar charts are best because they are the simplest. Use different colors to highlight the bars. Make sure your graphs are uncluttered. Do not have too many bars or pie sections. Also, on the graph, move from the largest item to the smallest – each category on the graph should be progressively smaller than the previous one or vice versa.

**Same Information – Different Impact**

| Type | 1990 | 2000 | 2010 |
|------|------|------|------|
| A | 100 | 110 | 150 |
| B | 80 | 100 | 170 |
| C | 70 | 90 | 120 |

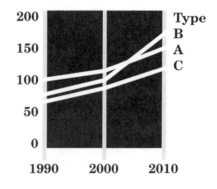

# Flow Charts and Schematic Diagrams

These are useful when describing a sequence of events or when outlining the relationship between several ideas. They can be used to illustrate a hierarchy of concepts, such as a corporate chain of command or different levels of authority. Also, divisions of corporate jurisdiction, or various segments of a market can be easily explained with charts. Be sure that your boxes and connecting lines in these charts accurately reflect the relationship between concepts.

In a corporate organization chart, for example, individuals of equal rank could be shown as parallel on a vertical hierarchy. Subordinates should be placed on the lower boxes of the hierarchy. Managers (including you and me!) are often sensitive to the level of their boxes relative to others.

**Customers**

**Employees talking with customers**

**Managers**

**In Reality:**

**Top Management**

**Top Management**

**As per Text Books:**

**Managers**

**Employees talking with customers**

# Cartoons

Humor always helps your presentation by humanizing it and adding variety. Cartoon visuals can be effective in dramatizing certain points you make. Usually, they tend to exaggerate a situation – either understating or overstating it. Humor softens the bluntness which helps get the point across. If you show a funny illustration every seven minutes, for just 15 seconds, you will be giving the audience a healthy mental break.

# Overhead Transparencies

Practice revealing the transparency on cue with the content of your speech. Keep the projector switched off until you are ready to reveal the transparency, then turn it on. Until you are ready to show the next one, keep the projector off. Shift the transparency. Then turn it on again.

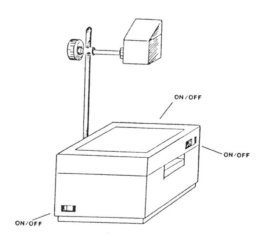

An alternative to switching the projector on and off, is to use a large sheet of thick paper or cardboard to blank out the entire screen of the projector until you are ready to reveal the transparency. When you change it, just lift the paper up to the lens of the projector. The audience will not see the change on the screen.

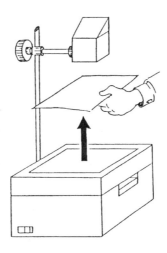

**Important:** Do not ever remove the transparency while the overhead projector is on! This will hurt the eyes of the viewers and looks very unprofessional!

## One Message Only

Ensure that overhead transparencies can be read easily. All the effort you put forth is pointless if the words are too small to be seen. The transparency – when not on the projector – should be readable, without straining, from a distance of six feet. If this is not possible, your type is too small. Make it larger. Have the overheads laser printed with attractive type.

Do not hand write them. It looks amateurish. Also, limit the text of each to six lines – no more than six words per line. Don't copy everything you are saying. If you do, why not give your audience a handout? Just provide a few key points. Less is more.

Use upper and lower case letters rather than block ones, as they're much easier to read. Do not write vertically as this is too difficult for your participants' eyes to scan. Use dark colors such as black, red, blue or green rather than orange, yellow and light brown. Pick shades which show at a distance. Mix different colors and type styles to highlight contrasting ideas.

Some effective transparencies are made on a blue or black background, with the words and pictures highlighted in yellow or white. There are courses available specifically on how to prepare and use overhead transparencies. 3M, for example, is one company that offers instruction.

## Write Notes on the Border of Your Overhead Transparencies

An effective technique to help you remember nitty-gritty details is to write all of the notes pertaining to a particular overhead transparency on the cardboard border and number them. Only you will know that you have them! Position the notes so that you can read them by glancing at the transparency as you face the audience.

Overhead notes are especially useful for things involving names, dates and descriptions. Why remember details if you do not have to? Write them down instead. (See diagram on opposite page).

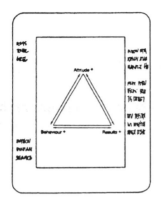

# Aligning Your Overhead Transparencies on the Screen

It is important that the transparencies you project are squared with the borders of the screen. Sometimes you end up with odd shaped images with one end larger than the other. Most of the time you can adjust the *screen* by tilting it toward or away from the projector. If the top of the image is wider than the bottom, tilt the top of the screen toward the projector. If the bottom of the image is too wide, move the top of the screen away from the projector.

# Do Not Show Them Everything At Once

As with handouts, do not show transparencies until you are ready. Isolate the parts of each one you wish to talk about and show it one line at a time. If you cover the transparency with a regular piece of paper, and turn on the projector, you can easily read through it to see the words as you stand near the projector. Meanwhile, the audience sees only what is not covered by the paper. You can start to talk about the ideas on the overhead before you reveal it and move smoothly from point to point.

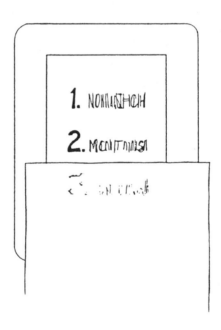

# Instaframe

This is a new gadget I recently discovered abroad. If you have a lot of loose transparencies to show, it can be very helpful. Place the Instaframe on the projector and put the first transparency in it. Adjust the frame's position until the picture in the screen is perfectly placed. Now you will have no problem with the remaining 100 loose transparencies. Just throw them into the Instaframe and they'll be perfectly aligned every time.

# Erasable Overhead Pens

If you write on your transparencies, and you plan to use them again, you could place an acetate overlay on top of each one. Or, instead use water soluble pens. Have the washable ones clearly marked. Do not mix them up with those used on the flipchart. I've seen people completely ruin their presentations because of that.

To be on the safe side, keep permanent non-washable pens away from the area where the transparencies are laid out and you won't risk using them.

# Organize!

If you intend to show several transparencies, have two piles: one for those you are about to present and another for those already used. Keep the "used" pile well away from the projector to ensure there is no confusion.

## Practice Your Handwriting

If you plan to write on your transparencies during your presentation, practice a few times in advance to ensure that it looks clean and tidy. Audiences hate sloppy writing. It distracts them. Practice will help you appear less nervous as you make notes. If you can't write neatly, prepare your overheads completely in advance and have them typeset.

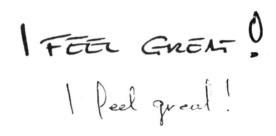

In general, large, thick writing implies greater confidence. Small, thin script makes you appear weak. If you are not a good speller, be extra careful. Pre-write your notes in advance on the border of the transparency, then just copy them onto the acetate as you go along. No one will see it except you! Another effective way to avoid spelling gaffes is to use abbreviations as often as possible.

However, if you have to write spontaneous notes (such as feedback from the audience) on a flip chart or white board, you might want to ask for an assistant. But if you are stuck doing it all yourself, have some one-liners ready in case you make an error. Try these:

*"I can't do two things at once – writing and spelling!"*
*"Any creative mind knows that there is more than one way to spell a word!"*
*"That's the American / Canadian / Swiss way of spelling it!"*
*"That's the way you spell it, I use olde Englishe"*

# Correct Positioning

It is important to use the hand closest to the projector when writing on the transparencies. If you are not ambidextrous (and most of us are not) you must, therefore, remember to position yourself on the side of the projector closest to your writing hand.

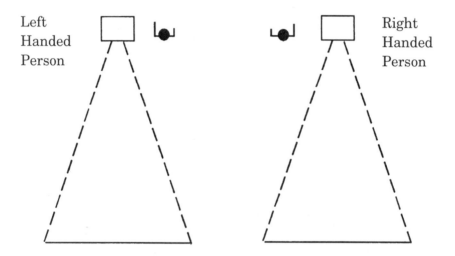

# When to Use Overhead Transparencies

These are best with audiences of between 10 and 400 people. Don't bother with them if you are presenting to fewer than ten people. Use handouts instead. If you give the same presentation repeatedly, an overhead projector comes in handy.

Another time to use it is when you have confidential ideas that you want to show your audience very quickly so they will be unable to completely reproduce them.

# Have a Back-Up Overhead Projector

If you give presentations to large groups and your message <u>depends</u> on overhead transparencies, I suggest you have a projector with two built-in light bulbs, or a back-up, to ensure that at least one works (so Murphy cannot get you!). Have the back-up ready and close by just in case your bulb burns out. While this might be extra work, it is a lot less stressful than stopping mid-way through your presentation and trying to change the bulb.

# Flipcharts

Whether professionally pre-printed or simple pads of plain paper, flipcharts are very useful. However, they are only good for groups of less than forty. Otherwise, the audience will not be able to read your message. Follow the "Five by Five Rule": never write more than five words across and five lines down. Use only the top two-thirds of each page so that the third row of the audience can still see everything.

Your handwriting must be extremely neat. If you cannot write clearly, have the charts professionally typeset in different colors with specialized lettering, logos, etc. The cost is minimal and the impact is tremendous. In preparing your presentation flipcharts, follow the K.I.L.L.E.M. Rule: Keep It Large, Legible, Exciting and Memorable.

# Preparation

Flipcharts can be great if you have all of your pages neatly prepared in advance. The advantage too is that you will not need note cards! You simply look at the charts as you go.

When referring to your flipchart, always talk facing the audience. Don't speak to your charts! Flip the page of paper away from view when not referring to it. Practice turning the pages of your preprinted flipcharts smoothly.

To help space your writing neatly and prevent errors in spelling, write down your points on each page of the flipchart faintly in pencil, in advance. Do this at home or at least one hour before your presentation. This process ensures that you will not forget anything. Your audience will not be able to see your pencilled-in notes and they'll be very impressed as you smoothly write out each point you talk about.

This is also effective if you must draw lines for a graph or possibly circles and squares. Personally, I am not very good at drawing but I'm great at painting by numbers and at following the pencil line! For diagrams, sketch all of the lines in advance using a compass and ruler. Then, just use different colored markers to follow the lines as you talk about the graph. Try it. It's easy and it looks great.

## Notes on the Back

If you have all of your charts written in advance, you can write detailed notes on the back of the chart so you can face the audience as you talk about each individual page. Position yourself about five feet behind the flipchart so you can glance at the notes any time. Only you need to know that you have them! Write them on the top reverse side of each page so you can read them easily as you stand behind the chart.

This technique is especially effective for dates, place names, descriptions and other tedious details. Take some time in advance to familiarize yourself with your notes. Simple preparation can instantly transform a novice into a top presenter. (See diagram on the next page).

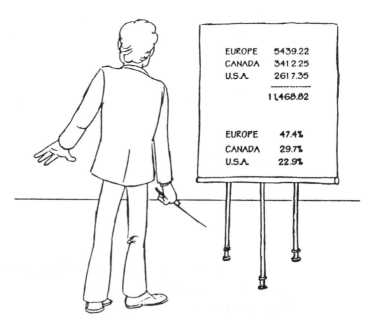

# Flipcharts to Gather Information

You might want to use flipchart pads to note audience feedback. Again, plan in advance. Anticipate the information you will get and plan how much space you'll need to use. The advantage of flipcharts for audience feedback is twofold: everyone can see the points that have been brought up, and there will be a permanent record of ideas which you can take away and refer to later on. This is helpful when you want to compare the responses of different departments or groups to the same ideas. Practice tearing pages off your flipchart pads. Use a sharp downward tug, or an elegant upward lift! You will need to do this if you are recording the information gathered from your audience.

# The Dual Chart System

A very effective technique is to use two separate charts. You can display contrasting ideas. For example, one can be used to list the advantages and the other, disadvantages. This is especially helpful when talking about complex, detailed subjects which are likely to result in much discussion. Use of the two-chart method will keep things more organized. Alternatively, one could be used for prepared ideas, while the other could be used to note creative thoughts arising spontaneously from the floor.

# Dark Colored Pens

When working with flipcharts, be sure that your writing is thick and dark. Light brown and yellow are very poor colors that can't be read easily at any distance. It is extremely important to test your markers in advance to ensure they are fresh. Always have extras in case they run dry as you write.

For contrast, you might want to use two different writing styles: block and script. For example, if you are reviewing a list of positives, write them with block letters. If you are listing negatives, use script. Contrast of some sort will help your audience visualize what you are talking about. Leave an extra page between each one worked on. Otherwise, your marking pens will soak through and damage your pre-printed pages.

When not writing on your flipcharts or for that matter on any visual, put your pen down so that you will not play with it and distract your audience.

## Right Handed – Left Handed

Be sure you stand on the correct side, when you write on the flipchart. Or even better, move the chart.

If you are right handed, the flipchart should be positioned to your left during the presentation. Thus, when you wish to write, move your body slightly to the left and you will be in perfect position to begin.

If you are left handed you should place the flipchart on your right . . .

## Using Flipcharts for Meeting Agendas: The Three Chart System

If you are chairing a meeting to discuss some business issues, a time saving way to ensure that everything stays on target is to use three flipcharts – each dedicated to a specific purpose during the meeting.

The first chart is the "master plan" and is reserved for all agenda points. This chart must be prepared in advance and the agenda should be agreed upon at the start of the meeting. It marks time intervals for the beginning and end of discussion on each point.

The second chart lists "who does what" and is reserved for action items which are agreed to during the meeting. When a participant commits to act on a particular agenda item, their name, the task and the deadline should be marked on the flipchart. There are three advantages to this:

1. It will be clear to all attending the meeting who has agreed to do what.

2. There will be a greater sense of accountability (it's in writing).

3. It will be clear toward the end of the meeting who has not yet volunteered to do anything. Thus, the workload in response to the agenda items will be fairer.

The third flipchart is for "Great Ideas" and should be used to retain all comments which are not quite relevant to the agenda items, yet still worth looking into. Recording these ideas on a special chart will ensure that they can be followed up at another time. Be sure to indicate who thought of the ideas as well!

The job of a skillful chairperson is to maximize the results obtained by the meeting participants. This technique ensures that everyone is kept on track and meetings are more productive.

The key to flipcharts, as with other visual aids, is advance preparation. Introduce the chart or transparency the very moment you plan to talk about the points noted on it. Use visual aids and flipcharts to save time and reinforce the audience's understanding of your verbal message.

# Tips for Effective Use
# of Flipcharts

- Move your flipchart into view only when you are ready to use it

- Test your markers in advance

- Use two charts to display contrasting ideas

- Never write more than five lines of five words

- Use only the upper two-thirds of each page

- Abbreviate words that are difficult to spell

- Pre-write your notes with pencil

- Stand on the "right" side, whether its right or left!

# Slides

These serve a purpose similar to overhead transparencies. However, the visual impact is far superior. They are especially suited to larger audiences. Slides allow you to show color photographs and prepared graphics in a much better way. A short, well-prepared slide show can be very powerful.

Be sure that your slides are aligned properly, right side up! There are eight different ways for a slide to fit into a carousel projector tray. Only one of these is correct! Check that *each* will be in focus. If your projector has an automatic focus, be sure that it works properly for each one. Otherwise, adjust it manually. Proper focusing and alignment is a must or your time will be wasted. Audiences get very irritated if they cannot read or see your message. Make it a regular practice to run through all of your slides in advance. Be sure, if the room is empty, to position your projector high enough so that heads do not block the image projected on the screen.

Your slides must fit your presentation or you should not use them. Whatever you present, explain what it is you are showing to the audience. Keep the slides moving at a fairly quick pace and pause in between. Know how to black out the projector between slides so that you can talk a bit more before moving on to the next frame. Most projectors do this automatically if you leave a blank space between each slide. Otherwise, use the company logo on a slide when you plan to pause. This will allow more time to explain your point before moving on to the next picture.

Have an organizing theme to all of your slides. Use the same background colors or symbols. This suggests to the audience that all of the images belong together. If your presentation is made to a corporation – your own or perhaps a client's, show a slide of the company's logo at the beginning and at the end of your show. Try to stress pictures rather than lines of text in your visuals. Choose images which explain the point you are making. Stick to one idea per slide. If you can, try to show some people who are familiar to the group. Another idea is to insert a shot of the city in which you are presenting. This creates comfort and trust between you and your listeners and helps personalize your presentation.

When preparing slides of text, use yellow or white lettering on a blue or black background. Mix and match colors as audience retention improves (up to 30%) over black and white.

Above all, ensure that all of your slides are readable from the back as well as from the front of the room. To ensure legibility, hold a slide at arm's length. If you can read the smallest type easily, it will be legible to your audience at a distance of eight times the height of the screen.

Also, try to keep all of your slides on the horizontal or the vertical rather than mixing them.

You could have your slides glass mounted. This will protect them from being scratched and from being burned when used in a heavy duty projector. They are also easier to keep clean.

## Remote Controls for Slide Projectors

These are essential for a smooth presentation. Most of the time your projector needs to be well back from the area in which you are standing in order for the image to appear large on the screen. Check that the cable on your remote is long enough. Otherwise, ask for an extension. Try out the connection.

Test the remote to ensure it is in working order. You must be able to advance and reverse through your slides easily.

Also, you should be able to control the focus of individual slides with your remote, unless your machine has autofocus capability.

Inevitably, one or more important pictures will need focusing while you are showing them. Learn to do this comfortably.

# Multimedia Shows

For sophisticated business presentations, you might want to prepare a fast paced multimedia show with a variety of moving and single framed images. I will not go in to detail here as there are many companies who design customized slide and visual shows. However, two slide projectors used in tandem can give you extra flexibility without necessarily costing a great deal of money – just some time in preparation.

Often, it's effective to show your primary slide on the left side of the screen with a secondary slide beside it on the right side. The secondary pictures can be used to provide details explaining the primary slides. For example, if you are describing the components of a manufactured part in different stages, you might show a slide of the finished product on the left with a slide highlighting one phase of production at a time on the right. The combinations of slides available to you are endless, yet the principle is the same: use one to illustrate a central point and another beside it to describe each subordinate point.

You will probably want to have an assistant to operate the projectors for you. A script, even a rough one is essential to ensure smoothness. It takes a <u>great deal</u> of practice to work with two slide projectors at a time!

# Films

These can provide a very powerful way of reinforcing your message. They can be most effective when making a longer presentation. Films cost a lot to create but are inexpensive to rent. Be sure that they fit your purpose and are appropriate for your audience's tastes and interests.

It is vital that you provide a proper introduction to the movie, clearly explaining your purpose in showing it and what you want everyone to gain from it. Do not ever just turn it on and expect the audience to figure out why you are showing it. Tell them what to watch for.

If there is something in the film that you think someone might object to, mention it in advance. Also explain that you think it is worthwhile in spite of the fact they might not agree with certain aspects.

Always preview a film you have not seen before showing it unless you really want to make a fool of yourself! Make notes regarding particularly important sections. Plan to draw the audience's attention to these points before and after your showing time.

We all tend to lose concentration during films, so it is important to capture and hold your group's attention. Without notice, stop the projector about three to five minutes into the show and talk about a point raised. Ask the audience a question to confirm their attention. If you suspect that a certain participant is not taking the presentation seriously, specifically call them by name and ask them if they understood what the film was saying. Then turn it on again. Everyone, from that point on, will pay great attention!

As with slide projectors, make sure the projector is positioned high enough that no one's head will block the movie. Make certain that you or someone else knows how to set up and run a film properly. Know how to thread the film, how to turn it on and how to rewind!

Libraries and other places lending audio visual equipment will often give short courses on the operation of projectors. Libraries in general are a great and inexpensive resource for educational films, videos and audio tapes.

When you are planning to screen a film, ensure that you have a take-up reel and especially one that is the correct size. Otherwise it will run off the reel and you will look like a clown.

# Video Cassette Recorders

The rules for these are similar to those for showing a film. However, VCRs are a lot simpler to use. It is important to ensure the tape is rewound and cued to the exact point you want to begin. Adjust the volume in advance – test to ensure it will be loud enough.

Carry a Video Head Cleaner Cassette with you; VCR equipment gets blurry from repeated use. Run the video head cleaner through before you show your video.

Practice with the VCR in advance until you can smoothly turn it on and off. Do not let the audience become distracted as you fumble around trying to begin.

Every machine is slightly different. Don't leave the group waiting impatiently for the tape to run. Twenty seconds spent waiting is like an eternity!

Be sure the VCR's clock is not flashing. This is very annoying to viewers. If you cannot fix it, cover it with your business card and some tape!

# Audio Cassettes

Cassette tapes can be very useful during a presentation, either for music, sound effects or recorded speech. Some presenters play a tape recorded introduction. Others just use up-beat background music to set the mood for the show. Sounds are always effective for entertaining speeches and any situation where you want a certain mood or a really dramatic effect.

Tape recorded interviews can be used quite creatively. For example, they are appropriate if you are surveying customer opinion or collecting testimonials about a new product. You can play a tape of different customers praising or criticizing the item. (It you don't like certain input, just erase it!).

This could be a great opener for a session on quality. Recorded references are very powerful and can enhance the credibility of any research data you present.

# Books

If you discuss a book or refer to some ideas from it, have a copy with you to show the audience. Hold it up high so they can see the front cover of it. Attach a 3 x 5 card on the back, with notes listing the key points you want to mention. Everyone will be amazed at your knowledge! Use "Post-it" notes to mark any chapters that you plan to quote. Do not use book marks. They always fall out at the wrong time and you'll look like a dunce trying to find the words of wisdom.

Clearly announce to the audience the full title, the author's name, the publisher and the ISBN number so they can easily track it down. Tell them where it can be purchased and the cost. Prepare this information on an overhead or flipchart so everyone can copy it. They will love you for the little added service you provide.

# Magnetic Whiteboards

A unique and effective way to construct diagrams and show pictures is to mount them with adhesive rubber magnetic tape and place them on a magnetized whiteboard. Lots of flipchart stands have these on the back. Rolls of magnetic rubber tape can be purchased in sophisticated office supply stores. All you have to do is gently place your "magnetized" pictures and charts on the whiteboard and they'll stay there until you take them off.

# Flourescent Dry-erase Markerboards

These writing boards have all of the same features as traditional whiteboards, except that they reflect with neon-like impact. The combination of bright, fluorescent colored markers writing on a ghost-like surface can be quite striking to the audience. Be careful to ensure your text is clearly visible.

# Chalkboards

There are still lots of these around. They are inexpensive, durable and effective. Just be sure that you have an eraser brush and lots of chalk. If your chalk squeaks – and most audiences cannot stand this – break it in half. This unpleasant noise comes from holding the chalk at too steep an angle. Try 45 degrees instead of 90. Another point to remember: Keep the chalk dust off of your dark clothes! Do not touch the blackboard with your sweaty hands! Avoid rubbing anything out by hand. Use a brush or towel.

# Reproducible Writing Boards

These are whiteboards which have an electronic scanner, similar to a photocopier, which can reproduce everything written down. This is quite useful for audience brain-storming as well as explaining complicated diagrams. The audience doesn't have to take notes and it ensures that everyone receives the message you wrote on the board.

# Pointers

Sometimes you will want to direct your viewers to certain

lines, words, symbols or pictures on a transparency, slide or flipchart. You might use a pointer which is like a telescoping radio antenna. These gadgets can be very helpful. However, if you play or fidget with them you will distract and annoy your audience. The oldest are the hardwood pointers of about two feet in length. Smack one of these around and old memories awake! The audience will start to listen carefully because now you are their old teacher.

There are also laser pointers which provide a thin red beam. These are great for highlighting. Your listeners might be impressed if they have never seen one.

The standard illuminated arrow pointer is a worthwhile alternative. These are like a small flashlight with a tiny arrow-shaped beam. Just be sure to check your batteries periodically to be certain it is workable.

If you use any kind of pointer, glance and move your body toward that which you are pointing. This signals your audience to look at the idea you are trying to explain.

## Pointers and Overhead Projectors

Instead of a hand held pointer for overhead transparencies you should use a solid object as a pointer and rest it on the projector over the transparency. Do not try to point on the screen. Use a letter opener or a square pen that will not roll off.

Another idea is to cut out a small cardboard arrow and rest it on the projector. This looks very professional and is inexpensive to do.

## Working with an Assistant

There are times when you require the use of so many visual

aids that you will need some help. If you do, be sure that you rehearse with that person in advance so that everything looks coordinated.

Train your assistant to reveal new slides on cue. Emphasize a quick pace so your auxiliary aid doesn't fall asleep! Be sure that you provide enough for your assistant to do. Otherwise, they'll look like they are on a game show!

## Confirm Your Equipment in Advance: Have a Back-up Plan

Order all of your equipment as soon as you know what you need. Confirm every item at least two days before show time. Note the name of the person who handled your confirmation.

Test to ensure that your projector bulbs work and that you have easy access to electrical hook-up. Organize extension cables. Test them.

Know where the breaker switches are in case you overload the power system with all of your electrical gadgets (Think about it, you might be using a microphone, an overhead and slide projector, all at the same time!).

Have the name and phone number of someone to call in case you have problems.

Always have a backup system hidden just in case something prevents you from using your planned visuals. Be prepared to go on and give an excellent presentation even without them. After all, airlines do lose luggage, fender benders happen, and you just might forget to bring something someday.

Plan ahead and look professional. Check the Comparison Chart for Use of Visual Aids on the following page.

| Type | Advantage | Disadvantage | Note |
|---|---|---|---|
| **Computer Aided** | Instant updates | System can crash | Always have alternate plan |
| **Overhead Transp.** | Good for groups of five or more Inexpensive | Looks clumsy if you use too many | Watch lighting 6 x 6 Rule |
| **Slides** | Quality images Efficient Reusable | Cost more Take time to prepare | Focus Make sure they are properly set in slide tray |
| **Flip Charts** | Pre-writing makes them easy to use Available everywhere | Too small for more than 40 people | Use top 2/3 of page only 5 x 5 Rule Practice your writing |
| **Handouts** | Inexpensive Flexible Easy to prepare | Take time to prepare | Must look professional Proofread |
| **Models** | Effective if notes attached | May get lost if passed around | Must be visible |
| **VCRs** | Stimulating Portable Easy to Use | Audiences drift | Preview Cue tape Set clock Off after 3 min. |
| **Films** | Stimulating to audience Often supplied free of charge by public libraries | Audiences drift tricky to run | Learn to run projector Take up reel Off after 5 min. |
| **White Boards** | Flexible Magnetic Can use Colors | Not too impressive Cost more Hard to erase | Write neatly Have eraser |
| **Chalk Boards** | Inexpensive Flexible | Not impressive Chalk squeaks Dirties clothes | Write neatly Have eraser |

# Summary
# Secrets on Effective
# Use of Equipment

- Confirm twice that all your equipment will be available on time at your location.

- Check and re-check lightbulbs, electrical power, cable connections, outlets and contacts, switches and any moving parts.

- Prepare your notes on your flip-charts and overhead transparencies at least three days before you make your presentation.

- Arrange to have back-up equipment close by and be prepared to present without visuals.

- Carry your overhead transparencies, slides and handouts (at least one) yourself to ensure they will not be lost.

*Rather fail with honor*
*Than succeed*
*by fraud*

*— Sophocles*

*To change one's thinking pattern,
Change the environment!*

*— PUB*

# THE FOURTH ESSENTIAL:

# THE ENVIRONMENT

The place and conditions in which you present have an important influence on how well your message is received. If the environment isn't right, participants won't pay the required attention and will become irritated.

To do a truly great job, it is very important that you be familiar with your presentation room in advance. Where will it be? Will you be in a board room at head office or a district branch? At a hotel, a college, or a conference centre? What facilities will be available?

Make every effort to visit the location so that you can determine what adjustments are necessary. Give yourself enough lead time for special arrangements as to seating, equipment, microphones, lighting and whatever you want to change.

## Location

If you have control over this, choose the city and site of your presentation carefully. I highly recommend that you spend more money obtaining the right environment and less on food and open bars.

A hotel is always better than your own board room. The neutrality of the location will help the audience concentrate on what you present rather than on unfinished tasks at the office. Make sure the site is easy for everyone to reach.

Send a detailed map well in advance, clearly indicating the name and address of the hotel, the presentation room and floor, the telephone number, the date and the exact time of the meeting. Try to ensure the hotel is close to main highways and the airport.

If you have an out of town site, check that there is adequate and (hopefully) free parking. Plan to park near the exit rather than the entrance so that you can leave quickly for your next meeting.

## Room Size and Layout

Know how many people will be attending your presentation and adjust the room accordingly. Be sure it's the right size – not too large or too small. Check that everyone will be comfortable and able to move easily. The best room dimensions are 1 x 1.5 deep, whatever measurements you use. It's essential that everyone can hear and see you without straining.

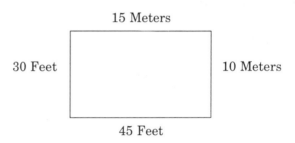

The layout should be conducive to your presentation and allow you to shift and glide around and have adequate space for your visual aids and projectors. Visit the room in advance. A hardwood rather than carpeted floor is better as it improves the acoustics.

Note the location of the nearest rest rooms and telephones so you can inform the audience. You will also need to know the room arrangement and arrive an hour early or perhaps the night before to completely arrange things as you like.

It is important that you feel 100% comfortable with the setting. If possible, rehearse part or all of your presentation there to get a feel for how it will go.

# Room Temperature

The room should be as cool as possible (without being uncomfortable) so that no one is likely to fall asleep. During the summer, adequate air conditioning is essential or you will sweat buckets! The room will become warmer once everyone arrives.

# Chairs

Arrange the chairs in advance into the fewest possible rows (see page 177) to suit your needs. Have soft chairs, but not too comfortable or participants will fall asleep! Most members of audiences tend to sit in the rows farthest back from the presenter, leaving the front seats vacant.

Mark the back rows with "reserved" signs, so that no one will sit there. As the room fills, you can remove the signs. Another idea is to put out fewer chairs than you will need, leaving the rest stacked at the back to be used as required.

It is important to have all audience members comfortably seated before you are introduced. The main thing to remember is that you want everyone situated so as to best hear and see your presentation. If you speak in a board room and know the names of the attendees, you might wish to pre-assign seating. It is better to position participants so they meet new people.

Arranged seating also reduces idle chatter. If your company's President or some other important business leader is expected to attend, plan to position them near the front where everyone, including you, can see their reaction to what you say. If the boss likes it, they will like it too!

For presentations involving note taking, you may want to furnish the audience with a writing surface where they can spread out notes, handouts, briefcases, etc. Each person should have a table space approximately 2.5 to 3 feet wide. You might want to supply notepaper, pens, mints, water, and other conveniences.

For presentations involving a screen, do not arrange chairs closer than twice the height of the screen.

Example: 10 foot screen – not closer than 20 feet.

3 meter screen – not closer than 6 meters.

The last row of seats should not be farther than eight times (8x) the vertical dimension of the screen.

Example: 10 foot screen x 8 – not farther than 80 feet.

## Barstools

These are great if you give a day-long presentation. You'll be glad to have a place to sit by 3 o'clock in the afternoon. Also, they provide the additional height and camouflage the fact that you are sitting.

## Doors

Make certain that the chairs are arranged so the doors are at the back of the room or at least the back corner. This will prevent latecomers from distracting the audience as they come in. Expect stragglers and do not allow them to interrupt you as you kick-off your presentation. If the doors are in the back, they can quickly be seated.

## Windows

It is also a good idea to locate these at the back of the presentation area (I know, it's hard to move them around!). Windows, especially if large, distract audiences. It is therefore important to present from the opposite side of the room, closing the curtains in advance to discourage wandering eyes.

# Styles for Room Set-Up

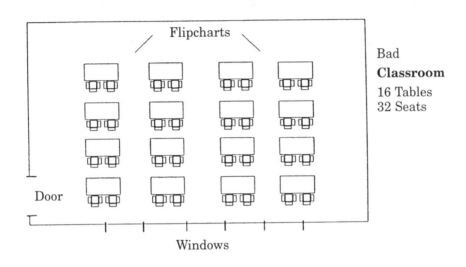

Flipcharts

Bad
**Classroom**
16 Tables
32 Seats

Door

Windows

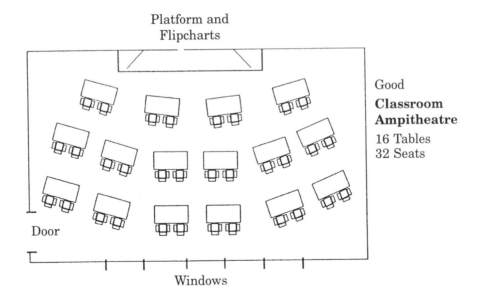

Platform and
Flipcharts

Good
**Classroom
Ampitheatre**
16 Tables
32 Seats

Door

Windows

# Styles for Room Set-Up

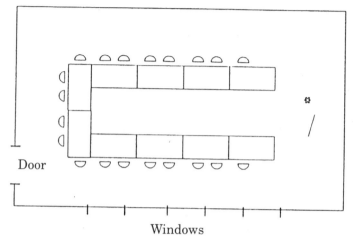

Bad
**U-Shape**
10 Tables
20 Seats

Door

Windows

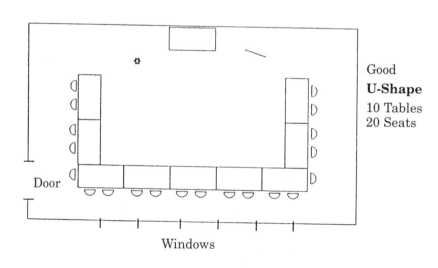

Good
**U-Shape**
10 Tables
20 Seats

Door

Windows

# Styles for Room Set-Up

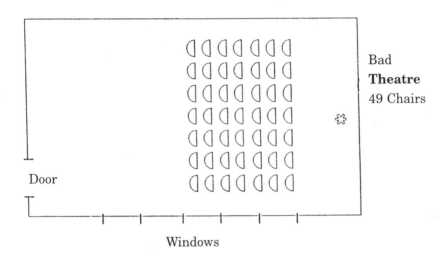

Bad
**Theatre**
49 Chairs

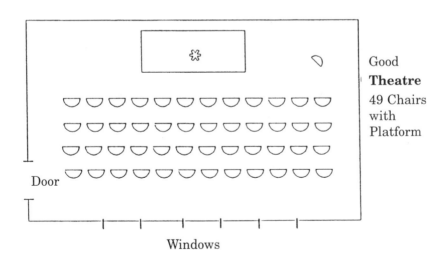

Good
**Theatre**
49 Chairs
with
Platform

# Lighting

Check out the room's lighting beforehand. Is it bright enough for everyone to see? Know where the switches are so that you can adjust as necessary. It's best if you can dim the lights rather than switch them off completely.

Locate your projectors so that you can turn the lights down without having to walk too far. Otherwise, cue someone to switch them down or up when you are ready.

Never allow yourself to be in complete darkness when using visual aids. It hurts the eyes and makes it hard for your audience to take notes.

An effective and dramatic illumination technique is to have the room dark before you begin, then turn the lights up completely when you start. This signals the audience to pay attention to your opening.

# Signs

For the convenience of your participants, place several signs clearly indicating the location of the meeting room. If the place is hard to reach, be sure there are posters and arrows in the lobby.

Also, double check that everyone is given accurate directions for finding your location by quizzing the front desk clerk. Pretend you do not know where to go (even if you do!) and find out if they are able to give you the correct information.

# Background Music

Check to see that the "elevator" music can be completely turned off. It is nice to have it before beginning but you must be able to turn it off. Locate the volume controls. Otherwise, it will ruin your presentation and annoy your audience.

# Timing

Be certain that your presentation is timed for greatest effect. Pick a time with minimal distractions from other events such as holidays, peak work periods, sporting events and other conferences.

It is also unwise to schedule meetings immediately before long weekends or vacation periods. Your audience might be with you in body but their minds will be somewhere else!

Plan to have breaks at periodic intervals (e.g. every 50/55 minutes) to allow your audience to move around, share feedback with other participants and absorb new ideas.

If you do not give a recess, they will fall asleep, get restless, and worse still, start to resent you. Know when to stop and offer a break. Regular stretches are also much appreciated during any long meeting.

# Emergency Exits

For the safety of your audience and yourself, check the emergency exit routes.

> *The price of greatness is responsibility.*
>
> — *Winston Chruchill*

# Suggested Breaks
## for a
## 8 a.m. to 4 p.m. Seminar

(If you really want the audience to work hard!)

*Duration*

| | | |
|---|---|---|
| 07:30 | Coffee, tea, juice, fruit, muffins and croissants | |
| 08:00 | Seminar begins | *50 min.* |
| 08:50 | Quick stretch (5 minutes) | *55 min.* |
| 09:50 | Coffee break for 15 minutes | *50 min.* |
| 10:55 | Quick stretch (5 minutes) | *50 min.* |
| 11:50 | Lunch for 1 hour. Keep it light. No alcohol | |
| 13:00 | Seminar reconvenes | *40 min.* |
| 13:40 | Quick stretch (5 minutes) | *40 min.* |
| 14:25 | Coffee, tea and assorted soft drinks for 15 minutes | *35 min.* |
| 15:15 | Quick stretch (5 minutes) | *40 min.* |
| 16:00 | Seminar ends | |
| | | *6 Hours* |

# Summary
# Secrets to Creating
# An Effective Environment

- Arrive at your presentation room the day before or at least one hour prior to your talk.

- Turn on the air conditioning or open all the windows to allow fresh air into the room.

- Know where all the light switches are hidden. Find out the purpose of all other switches on the walls so you do not touch the wrong ones.

- Put out fewer chairs than you know will be used. Stack the rest at the back of the room.

- Put a "Reserved" sign in the last row of chairs to encourage people to sit close to the front.

- Close the curtains.

- Locate all telephones in your presentation room and arrange to have them disconnected or call forwarded to another extension.

- Rearrange whatever you must in order to feel comfortable in the room.

*If I had eight hours*
*to chop down*
*a tree*
*I'd spend six*
*sharpening my axe.*

*— Abraham Lincoln*

PREPARATION – Speech – Body Language – Equipment – Environment –

*Before everything else, getting ready is the secret of success.*

*— Henry Ford*

# THE FIFTH ESSENTIAL:

# PREPARATION

**P**reparation is the final step that brings the other four essential elements of your presentation together. If you do not prepare, you are playing Russian roulette! Good preparation compensates for lack of talent.

However, failure to plan in advance combined with the absence of talent can destroy your credibility. So, be prepared. As the saying goes,

### *"Perfect Prior Preparation Prevents Poor Performance!"*

Order all the equipment you need well in advance. Know the name of the person who booked it for you and make note of it. Find out who else might be involved in using your equipment the day you will present. If you need help or if there is a mix up, refer to those responsible immediately. Arrange for back-ups. Confirm again all your requirements the day before you present.

If you send your own equipment and handout materials to the presentation location, be sure you do this well in advance. Mark the box or case in which you shipped them with bright unusual colors or easy to remember symbols, such as Mickey Mouse or your national flag (mine often has a Swiss cross on it). Confirm that the packages you send actually arrived. But to be on the safe side, take the essential items with you in your car or in your hand-carried luggage right on the plane.

## Don't Complain If Things Aren't Perfect

If you had time to organize and make special arrangements and you didn't, don't complain. Now it's too late! You have no one to blame but yourself.

If you do not like the room you are assigned, say so at the very beginning and see about getting another. If you cannot change it, live with it. Don't grumble, mumble and complain. It will not help you get ready.

## Travel Tips for Presenters

Give yourself enough time to reach your destination. Allow for unexpected traffic and bad weather. It only snows when it shouldn't and Murphy only orders freezing rain on important days.

Arrange to have someone meet you at the airport. Write that person's name and telephone number down in your diary

Never take the last possible plane before your presentation time, but instead, leave early enough so that you can rely on a later flight in the event of a cancellation.

Carry the minimum presentation materials and clothing with you in the plane. If the other luggage gets lost, you will at least have the essentials to go ahead with your presentation unruffled.

If you travel alone by car, have clear, explicit directions.

## Send Thank You Notes to the People Who Will Help You, In Advance

It is critical that your presentation goes smoothly. Take every precaution to see that nothing can go wrong. You always need to depend on others to a certain extent to help you achieve this. Show them that you appreciate their assistance and that you are depending on them to help make you look good. Be genuine.

Send a short note or post card to everyone who has helped you with booking arrangements. If you have any special requests the day of your presentation or if there is an emergency, these people will go the extra mile for you.

# Publicity

Be certain that either you or your meeting organizer announce the topic, date, location, and time of your presentation well in advance. If someone else is doing the promoting, at least know what was said or written about you.

Attendance is critical: if you are the only one to show up, your preparation is a waste. Also, if your session is away from the normal working environment, be sure the recommended dress code is clearly announced. Everyone should know what to wear – whether it be suits, casual clothes or summer shorts.

# Body Language

If you've put on a bit of weight, attempt to shed it. (As of now, not Monday!) Tell yourself how good you look. Get a haircut one week in advance – not the day before. Wear your favourite suit, dress, tie or scarf providing it is appropriate for your audience. Get a good night's rest. Do not drink alcohol within 24 hours of your presentation. Not because of hangovers... because of dehydration.

# Rehearse, Rehearse, Rehearse

Do not practice with your staff. They will only tell you how good you are – even if you aren't! If you make mistakes they will be too polite to tell you. (But, they'll laugh their heads off later). Instead, drill with your peers – they are tougher and will give you honest feedback.

Rehearse your opening and closing – know them inside out. Be sure that they are written out. Time yourself. Do it in front of a mirror to get your gestures just right.

Above all, if possible, rehearse in front of a real audience, such as a professional group or service club before the target date. If you give a sales presentation, do it a few times for other clients before you take on your best prospect.

Practicing before a real audience, in advance, allows you to make minor mistakes and work out any bugs. They will challenge you under actual conditions.

You'll be able to make corrections in time for the Big Day and therefore have a good idea as to likely timing, best use of visual aids, and probable questions and objections. The more audiences you present to, the more prepared you will be for your Big Day.

However, if you just can't find "real audiences", be sure you practice on your feet. Yes, on your feet! Sounds simple, but there is a big difference.

Standing erect will bring optimum results in terms of breathing and body language. You will feel a lot more comfortable.

# Presentation Speed

85% of presenters begin too fast. Here is an exercise to help slow you down:

– Visualize yourself for thirty seconds opening your presentation as *fast as you can*, with *full animation*, in your *loudest voice* and with *too much excitement*.

– Then, visualize yourself for another thirty seconds slowing down to a *dead crawl*, speaking *very slowly* with *no emotion*, and a *very low voice*.

Having done this, you may now have an idea of the range of speed requiring adjustment. Slow yourself down to just the right speed. Work on this during rehearsal. Remember, it is better to go slower than faster as this will make you look far more confident. Also, be sure you incorporate some appropriate long pauses between sentences, particularly at the beginning.

> ***Silence is the ultimate weapon of power***
>
> *– Charles de Gaulle*

## Staying on Time

Mark your notes to remind yourself of the time. Have someone in the audience cue you at strategic points near the end of your presentation. Never go overtime.

Be known as a speaker who begins on time and ends on time! Always have a clock, but one that cannot be seen by the audience. Check the time often, as discreetly as you can.

# Visual Aids
# Transparencies, Handouts, Slides, etc.

Have these ready several days before you present. Show samples to potential audience members to get their reaction. Make changes if necessary.

Use colored paper for handouts instead of white. Choose a professional looking type style rather than plain old typewriter. Have your handouts ready to distribute at the right time.

Help prepare your audience for notetaking. Tell them what to write down. If they are learning, they should take notes as they listen to you. If you are giving general information, they can wait until you pass around the handouts.

We all appreciate it when a speaker tells us which ideas are most important and which are not, so that we know what to remember.

# "Reserved" Signs

At annual company dinners, or when entertaining large groups of customers and prospects, 10 – 20% of the seats are always empty. The same, of course, applies to early breakfast sessions and other large gatherings.

No one wants to sit at the front and often you find quite a few half-filled tables. This does not encourage people to become acquainted, nor does it help the speaker communicate.

Get some "Reserved" signs and place them on the rear tables so everyone must move closer to the front.

The same technique, of course, can be used for theatre-style presentations. Just block off the last few rows with a colorful rope and "Reserved" signs.

You might present in a board room where there are always more chairs than participants. Remove the excess chairs before the troops arrive. This way you create a better meeting atmosphere.

## Talk to Participants in Advance

If you address an unknown audience, telephone three people who will be attending a few days in advance and ask them what they hope to gain.

Familiarize yourself with their backgrounds and ask them to tell you more about the rest of the group if they can. What are their problems and how can your presentation help them? If you are a total stranger to the group, try to discover the important, unwritten, group "rules" if possible.

Be sure that you do not accidentally offend anyone. Know what the audience members like and dislike and prepare accordingly.

# Daily Exercises
# to Help You
# Improve Your Voice

- Practice deep breathing through your nose into your diaphragm. Your stomach should rise as you fill up with air. Think of making yourself fat!

- Slow down your rate of speech. The slower you speak, the deeper your voice will sound.

- Breathe deeply as you go to sleep, drive your car or wait in the boardroom.

- Repeat the following aloud several times, clearly pronouncing each syllable: "Lah, Lee, Lie, Low, Lu". Repeat, lowering your voice each time.

If you catch your voice cracking, stop speaking and swallow. Have a pitcher of warm water close by – not cold and especially with no ice. Cold water causes your vocal cords to contract, making your voice less flexible. It's best to take a quick sip of water before you need it. Try to drink when the audience is not watching you. Ask them to view a visual or write something down.

Do not drink milk or coffee with cream before or during your presentation! The milk in the coffee will dry up your saliva and make your mouth gummy and can cause your voice to crack.

Do not eat ice cream, cheese or other dairy products either as these will have the same effect. So does toothpaste. Soft drinks with sugar are not good for your voice either. Warm water or plain tea is best.

> *If you do not conquer self,*
> *You will be conquered by self.*
>
> *– Napoleon Hill*

## Using Your Voice Effectively

One of the most powerful tools you have as a presenter is your voice. There is a great interdependence between the way you use it, how you breathe and the confidence you feel. This relationship is illustrated on the following page:

# How Breathing Influences the Impression You Make

| **Good** | | **Bad** |
|---|---|---|
| Slow/Deep Relaxed | **– BREATHING –** | Fast/Shallow Uptight |
| Low/Warm | **– VOICE –** | High/Shaky |
| Confident | **– SUBCONSCIOUS –** | Insecure |
| "I can" "I am great!" | **– SELF ESTEEM –** | "I can't" "I am a fool!" |
| Comfortable Calm | **– BODY LANGUAGE –** | Stressed Fidgety |
| In Full Control | | Nervous, Uncertain |

**TOTAL IMPRESSION**

**PROFESSIONAL**          **UNPROFESSIONAL**

# How to Introduce a Speaker

What is involved in a good introduction? Again, think about what the audience wants and needs to hear. Get that information right out in the open. Grab their attention and explain that you will be talking about something of great interest to them.

Here are the three steps to an effective introduction:

## I. Establish the importance of the subject

Create a context and give a concrete example of the subject so the audience can relate. This could be a new idea attracting wide interest or possibly a problem that requires a solution. For example:

> *"These days in business, **what** you say is not as important as **how** you say it. Words account for only a small part of the total message we convey to others. The rest comes from our **style**, use of voice, body language, and other non-verbal forms of communication."*

## II. Relate the subject to the audience's interests at that particular moment

In a business situation, the listeners will probably have particular goals and objectives. Explain how the subject will help the members of your audience reach their goals. Spell out precisely, "what's in it for them". Here is an example:

*"As a manager, you will soon have to make more presentations to get your point across clearly. The success of XYZ as market leader depends on our ability to **communicate effectively** with our customers as well as our employees. To remain competitive all our managers must become first class presenters."*

### III. **Highlight the speaker's qualifications to present on that topic**

Say things that are true and relevant to the listeners. Never lie or stretch the truth. However, downplay any negatives or turn them into positives. There may be things about you that the audience will not like such as having worked for a competitor or holding membership in a profession that is at odds with them.

As in the rest of your presentation, stress similarities between you and your audience first, then differences.

See the opposite page for a complete sample introduction which I use for seminars on "Presentations".

**A good introduction
is short, precise
and
to the point.**

# Sample Introducton:
# "Peter Urs Bender On Presentation"

### (Importance of Topic)

*These days in business, what you say is not as important as how you say it. Words account for only a small part of the total message we convey to others. The rest comes from our style, use of voice, body language, and other non-verbal forms of communication.*

### (Relate the Topic to the Audience)

*As a manager, you will soon have to make more presentations to get your point across clearly. The success of XYZ as market leader depends on our ability to communicate effectively with our customers as well as our employees. To remain competitive all of our managers must become first-class presenters.*

### (Qualifications of Speaker to Lecture on the Topic)

*Our speaker and seminar leader, Peter Urs Bender, is an expert in business presentations. He has worked with many companies to improve the communication skills of both managers and sales people. He has lectured across North America, Europe, and the Far East on the topic of "Effective Presentations". He also is the author of "Secrets of Power Presentations".*

*We look forward to hearing the many new ideas he has to share with us today. Let us all join in welcoming to XYZ Company, Peter Urs Bender....*

Provide your introduction double-spaced on a single sheet of paper. Put in commas for easy breathing and underline the words you want accented.

Take the time to prepare a written introduction of yourself and your topic in the three-step way described. It can make a world of difference to the impression created before you even open your mouth.

Do it right now, take a few minutes. Read it aloud listening to how good it sounds. Be sure you have it for your next presentation.

Do not take the risk of getting a bad or an average introduction (where they talk about your 2.3 kids and the 1.4 spouses to whom you are happily married).

To ensure 100% co-operation, the following message accompanies my introduction:

*(DEAR FRIEND): This professional introduction was developed so as to assure an effective and enjoyable presentation for the audience, and enhance the message of the speaker. Please DO NOT deviate from it by adding personal remarks (as: I have been asked to read this) or by omitting any part. Experience has shown that the quality of a professional speaker's introduction by his introducer, YOU, influences how receptive the audience will be to the material presented. Please co-operate by using this written introduction and thereby ensure a professional worthwhile experience for yourself, the audience and the speaker.*

# Preparing for Questions

The question and answer period is when the "real" you shows up. Be at your best. Audience questions provide you with another opportunity to emphasize your points, clarify your ideas and zero-in on what the listeners are most interested.

Responding effectively and intelligently at this time will make you look professional. The secret is to prepare in advance.

There are many situations where you will be expected to answer questions:

- Presenting a budget proposal to your superiors
- During a training session with staff
- When meeting the press
- During labor/management negotiations
- Presenting a proposal to prospective clients
- During a regulatory hearing
- When introducing a prototype for a new product
- During a panel performance evaluation session

The best and only way to get the most from these situations is to anticipate in advance all questions that will likely arise. Depending on your topic, the audience might have objections to your claim, point out problems they want help with, or ask you to comment on their own ideas. Some people will aggressively challenge you.

It is important to develop responses in advance, especially with negative feedback, so you won't be caught off guard by the tough questions. Ask others to role play when forming ideas on difficult questions and how to handle them. Get them to coach you as you rehearse.

Reserve some of your material for the question-and-answer session of your talk. That way you'll still have some new things to say after you have completed the main part of your presentation. But let the audience raise the points first. You are thus able to portray yourself as someone able to think on your feet, when you were actually prepared in advance. That is what preparation is all about. Nothing should be a surprise.

> *The wise man*
> *avoids evil*
> *by anticipating it*
>
> *— Publilius Syrus*

## Get the Questions You Want

Plant some thought provoking questions in advance. Write each one on a 3 x 5 card and give them to friendly participants. Tell them to ask those questions on cue. Do not give them to participants sitting in the front.

When you are ready, you will cue: "Do you have any questions?" This technique is good for starting a question-and-answer routine. When trying it, select (if possible) participants who have deep voices, project well, look good, have an honest appearance and sit in the back!

If you have trouble generating feedback, ask: "Do you have any other questions?" or volunteer one yourself saying: "One of the most commonly asked questions about this is..." or "I thought you might ask about..."

# Take Questions From Groups

A very helpful technique is to organize your audience into groups of three or four and have them devise one or two questions.

The groups tend to screen out those which are too basic or silly and think of very thought provoking responses instead. Your discussion of these questions will be very rewarding and interesting to everyone concerned.

# How to Answer Questions

Always maintain eye contact with the questioner while they are talking. Indicate with your body language that you are concentrating on them alone. Nod your head. Smile softly. Keep your eyes open. Slowly *walk away* from the questioner.

You will create an "electrical field" between you and the questioner. The bigger the field, the more electricity is in the air. Keep eye contact with everyone in the room so each person will feel included.

Whenever a participant asks you a question, be sure to repeat it slowly and loudly so that everyone will hear it. This will ensure total audience understanding. More importantly, doing this will make the questioner feel good and give you more time to think of your answer!

# Thank Participants for Their Questions

Always begin by thanking the individual asking the question. If it is not constructive or if you disagree with the comment made simply say "thank you for your feedback". At all times, make the questioner feel important.

As a presenter, you want the audience to respond to you.

Reward them when they do. Never, ever make someone feel foolish in front of a group, especially not in front of their peers.

## Focus on Areas Of Agreement

Isolate audience objections and place them in the proper perspective. Balance objections with points that outweigh them. Accent the positive and minimize the negative. Ask for clarification on points of agreement. Have the participant clarify the extent of their objection. Seek to understand the questioner's point of view even if you do not agree. Say things like:

> *"I understand what you are saying, however it is my view that..."*

> *"That is a tough question. (Pause. Nod your head. Look serious. Bite your lips slightly while you think), Wouldn't you agree that...."*

> *"I understand what you are asking, and that leads to an even more important question...."*

> *"That's true. However I believe your concern is out- weighed by the fact that..."*

## When to Answer

It is usually best to deal with questions as they arise. Don't ask the audience to wait. But if you do promise to answer the questions later, be sure that you do. Tell them at the beginning how you plan to take questions. Invite them to participate. Be genuine. We all feel somewhat threatened by asking questions in front of others. Make everyone feel comfortable doing it.

If it appears that you made a mistake during your presentation or if you stumbled making a point, simply try again. Say things like:

> *"I'm sorry I wasn't clear about that point. What I meant is..."*

> *"Let me clarify what I meant by that...."*

**Never** blame the audience if they didn't understand you! You just didn't make yourself clear. Do not say things like: "I just showed you that. Didn't you see it?" or "You don't understand?!"

## Special Situations During Question and Answer Sessions

Long-winded questions – Be patient. Maintain eye contact and open body language. Say:

> *"Let me try to summarize that..."*

Personal questions – Respond:

> *"I do not believe that is a fair question" or "That is a personal question that I don't wish to answer".*

Try rephrasing the question in more appropriate terms, say:

> *"Let me restate your question. What you are asking ....Is that the question?". "Really, your question is about..."*

Never say, *"No comment"*. This suggests that you have something to hide. It also sounds rude.

The final rule about questions: Always **be honest**.

> ## No man has a good enough memory to make a successful liar.
>
> — *Abraham Lincoln*

If you do not have an answer say so. Promise instead to find out for the person. Get their address and telephone number and get back to them with the missing information. Say this:

> *"That is a very good question. I'm sorry but I do not know the answer right now. I will do my best to find out for you. Could you leave me a number where I can contact you tomorrow? I am interested in finding out about it right away...."*

Audiences will love you for that, as long as you do not answer every question that way!

If you get a really unusual or tough question, honestly say something like this:

> *"Do you know that in all of my years with the company you are the first person who has ever asked about that!*

> *"That is very interesting. No one has ever asked me that before."*

> *"Really. I've never heard of that happening before..."*

These are all effective responses.

# Handling Negative Interruptions from your Audience

Unfortunately, for reasons which are not your fault, there are times when you will not have the full attention of your listeners. You might encounter a member of the audience who frustrates your ability to present your ideas.

There are two rules you must remember:

**First**, under no circumstances should you lose your cool, become upset or get angry with that person.

**Second**, recognize that the audience will almost always be your ally if you are harassed or heckled. Everyone will be as annoyed as you are and encourage you to continue.

Therefore, the best way to handle inconsiderate interruptions is to just ignore them and keep going. If that fails, try one of the following techniques:

## Hecklers

Ignore them. Do not make eye contact. If all else fails, try one of these lines: "Excuse me but I work alone". Ask them to be quiet or leave. Stop your presentation until they do. If you suspect in advance that you might have hecklers, arrange for two allies to assist you.

If a certain person persists in harassing you, have your two friends escort the person out of the room to take a telephone call.

Outside, your helpers can politely ask the person to be more considerate as you continue your presentation.

## Silly questions

Say, "That's interesting, thank you for your feedback." Ignore them and move on.

## Hostile remarks

Ignore them. Do not get angry or hot under the collar.

## Latecomers

Ignore them. Tape the door latches open so that noise is reduced.

## Telephone calls

Disconnect all telephones in the room. Have reception hold all calls and take messages for participants. Do not allow people to be called out of your presentation to answer the telephone.

## Pagers

Ask the audience members having them to turn them off or leave them in the lobby.

## Portable telephones

Same as pagers. Ask participants to turn them off and leave them in their briefcases.

## Chatterers

Call them by name and politely ask them to be quiet. If they persist, say: "I'm sorry but we can only have <u>one</u> meeting at a time...."

# Smart Alecks

Have the name of the employee of the month, star manager, or top producer of the company written on a notecard. Memorize it. If interrupted, call the offender by that name, saying: "Oh, you must be . . . . . . . . . . I've heard all about you! Why don't you come up and tell us more about how you'd do this....".

# Conclusion: What's in it for You and What's in it for Them

Ultimately, the key to a powerful presentation is to be conscious of your objective. Remind yourself what's in it for them. How will the audience benefit from listening to you? Knowing the benefits of what you have to say will give you greater confidence.

# What's In It For You

Presenting is one of the most exciting challenges you'll ever take on. You are in a unique position to share your ideas and experience with others. Mastery in presenting to one group will inevitably lead to even greater triumphs before future audiences.

However, one thing is certain, if you give a bad presentation, everyone will talk about it and word will get around fast! Unfortunately – unless you are an outstanding presenter – even if you give a good presentation, your audience will not necessarily tell everyone how good you are. That's life. It's up to you to recognize when you've done your best and know those areas where you can still improve. Sometimes things will go wrong. Preparation and a positive mental attitude will help you minimize the negative impact of such occurrences.

Now you know all of my secrets. Actually, I have one more:

If you look at all the accomplishments of the greats of history, you can see that it's not what you know but what you do with *what* you know that makes the difference. Great things happen not because of knowledge alone but through the persistent pursuit of a clearly defined goal.

Thus, the final secret is:

> # Do it!
> # Do it now!
> # Do it often!

Knowledge is power, there is no question. But it is useless if not applied. It is more important to do the *right* job and less important to *just* do the job right!

# Old Speeches

Keep a file somewhere in your office, where you can store presentations you have given. After a short time, two to three years, you can start to recycle quite a bit of the old material.

Always remember, it is easier to find a new audience than to create a new speech.

Just look at yourself – where were you three years ago? Are you still surrounded by the same people, in the same department, in the same company? The answer is probably no. Therefore, in a short time you will again have new faces all around you and no one will have heard your old presentation. And if they did, they will have forgotten most of it anyway!

# Twenty Percent Change

If you are able to modify one fifth of a presentation to suit the particular situation, you more or less have a custom designed show. You do not have to re-invent the wheel every time.

Remember, your audience is forever changing and as human beings we do forget. As long as you make some changes your message will continue to captivate.

*Success comes before work . . .*
*but only in the dictionary!*

# Summary
# Secrets of Worthwhile
# Preparation

- Rehearse your speech while standing on your feet.

- Learn to start slowly and practice.

- Have a hidden clock.

- Make use of "Reserved" signs.

- Warm up your voice daily.

- Have a written introduction.

- Prepare for your question period.

- File your used speeches for later reference.

Speech – Body Language – Equipment – Environment – Preparation –

# APPENDIX

*I am a great believer in luck
and find the harder I work
the more I have of it.*

*— Stephen B. Leacock*

# Checklist for the Prepared Presenter

## Three Days
## Before Your Presentation

- Know your message in point form. Write it on cards. Summarize the objectives of your presentation in one sentence.

- Practice your opening and closing statements. Write each out on a separate 3 x 5 card. Keep some blank cards on hand in case you need them.

- Rehearse your presentation 3 times on your feet and if you can, rehearse in front of a "test audience".

- Prepare sample audience questions and answers for each. Write some of them down on 3 x 5 cards to be planted with members of the audience.

- Finish preparing all of your overheads and flipcharts. Practice working with them. Be sure they are readable.

- All of your handouts should be finalized and copies made. Print 10% more than you need. Use one file folder for each handout.

- Confirm that all equipment is booked for the room you will use. Have a contingency plan in case the equipment doesn't arrive.

- If possible, check out the room in which you will speak a week before hand. Find out how much rearranging you will need to do. Draw a diagram.

- Prepare a powerful introduction for yourself, to be given by another person. Write it out in full, to be read by the introducer word for word.

- Pick out the clothes you will wear. Be sure that they have been properly cleaned.

- Practice deep-breathing exercises so that you will be relaxed and in control at the time of your presentation.

- Visualize your audience. See everyone smiling at you, eagerly and with anticipation! Visualize their expressions changing as you speak to them. See them applauding and laughing at your one-liners.

- Be animated and enthusiastic when you present. But adapt to the audience. Be just a bit more enthusiastic than they are.

- Add drama and energy to your presentation. Practice saying these words over and over to yourself:

> *"I feel like taking on whole armies*
> *by myself...*
> *I have ten hearts. I have 100 arms.*
> *I feel too strong to war with mortals.*
> *Bring me GIANTS!"*.

216

# Checklist for the Prepared Presenter

## 24 Hours
## Before Your Presentation

- Be sure that your briefcase is packed with:
  - An introduction, written out in full for someone else to read.
  - Prepared overhead transparencies or flipcharts.
  - Prepared handouts – wrapped to keep them clean.

- Know exactly how to get to your speaking location. Leave enough time in case you get lost, take the wrong highway exit, or become stuck in traffic! Have a plan in case your car breaks down!

- Know the names of your contact meeting organizers. Be sure that you have their telephone numbers handy in case of last minute problems with the presentation arrangements.

- Know the names of important people attending your presentation. Practice their names. If you can, find out something about them you can mention if and when you run into them.

- Bring felt markers, overhead pens, pencils (for handout exercises), whiteboard pens and eraser, chalk and a chalk brush. Do not assume the meeting room will have these things.

- Pack models and other special display material in a special case to avoid breakage.

- Be sure that your car is gassed up and clean (We always feel better when driving a nice, clean car!)

- Polish your shoes and have your clothes ready.

- Practice the presentation one more time.

- Always have a Plan B. Ask yourself, "What's the worst thing that could go wrong?". Know what you'll do in case the worst happens.

- Remember, it's only a presentation; it's not brain surgery! Relax!

Tell yourself over and over:

**I work for the
best company!**

**I work for the
company with the
best service!**

**Today
I am the best
presenter ever!**

# Booking Arrangements for your Presentation

- Announce your presentation as soon as the dates are confirmed. Give people as much advance notice as possible. Confirm the location.

- Announce the presentation topic and its significance to the audiences. Stress the benefits of your ideas and how you will help the participants meet their goals or solve their problems.

- Publicize yourself and your background credentials well in advance. Get the organizers to do it for you, but give them biographical material with which to work. Get others to establish your credibility.

- Be sure that the meeting facilities will be appropriate for the size of the gathering and the tone you wish to set. The room should not detract from the objectives you have set.

- If appropriate, plan to serve a light, low-cost lunch, such as soup and salad. Don't serve alcohol. For break fast sessions, serve coffee, tea, juice, muffins, croissants. Do not serve sweet danishes or donuts as sugar will cause your listeners to get a quick high and then fall asleep.

- Ban smoking from the meeting area. Hide all the ashtrays in advance. If necessary, provide a place for smokers to use during breaks.

- Arrange name tags. Clearly display the first name of the participant. Have them handed out at the entrance to your meeting room.

- Mix assigned seating of the audience to encourage interaction. People who know each other should be discouraged from sitting together.

- Appropriate dress for participants should be publicized well in advance. Make it very clear whether your presentation requires formal or casual clothing.

- Changes in presentation location or numbers of participants should be reported to you and the invited guests no less than 48 hours in advance.

- Give out evaluation forms at the end of the presentation to get audience feedback. Include questions such as: What are the three best ideas you gained from the presentation? How do you plan to implement them? How might you improve the content and delivery of the presentation?

*Love your enemies,*
*for they tell you your faults.*
*— Benjamin Franklin*

# THE ACHIEVEMENT GROUP
## WORKSHOP EVALUATION

### Date:_____

Use the following ratings as you answer each question

5 Very Good        4 Good        3 Satisfactory        2 Poor        1 Very Poor

A)  How effective was this session?                                    _____

B)  Rate this workshop as a personal experience                        _____

C)  How useful will the ideas be in your job?                          _____

D)  Would you recommend this workshop to others                        _____
    To whom?

_____

_____

_____

E)  What specifically did you enjoy the most about the workshop?

_____

_____

_____

F)  What could be improved?

_____

_____

_____

G)  On what subjects should we have spent more time?

_____

_____

_____

# How Much Do Meetings Really Cost?

## One Hour Meeting

## Number of Participants

| Average Hourly Cost Per Participant* | 2 | 4 | 6 | 8 | 10 | 15 | 20 | 50 | 100 |
|---|---|---|---|---|---|---|---|---|---|
| $10 | 20 | 40 | 60 | 80 | 100 | 150 | 200 | 500 | 1000 |
| $20 | 40 | 80 | 120 | 160 | 200 | 300 | 400 | 1000 | 2000 |
| $30 | 60 | 120 | 180 | 240 | 300 | 450 | 600 | 1500 | 3000 |
| $40 | 80 | 160 | 240 | 320 | 400 | 600 | 800 | 2000 | 4000 |
| $50 | 100 | 200 | 300 | 400 | 500 | 750 | 1000 | 2500 | 5000 |
| $60 | 120 | 240 | 360 | 480 | 600 | 900 | 1200 | 3000 | 6000 |

## Cost if you Start 12 Minutes Late!

| Average Hourly Cost Per Participant* | 2 | 4 | 6 | 8 | 10 | 15 | 20 | 50 | 100 |
|---|---|---|---|---|---|---|---|---|---|
| $10 | 4 | 8 | 12 | 16 | 20 | 30 | 40 | 100 | 200 |
| $20 | 8 | 16 | 24 | 32 | 40 | 60 | 80 | 200 | 400 |
| $30 | 12 | 24 | 36 | 48 | 60 | 90 | 120 | 300 | 600 |
| $40 | 16 | 32 | 48 | 64 | 80 | 120 | 160 | 400 | 800 |
| $50 | 20 | 40 | 60 | 80 | 100 | 150 | 200 | 500 | 1000 |
| $60 | 24 | 48 | 72 | 96 | 120 | 180 | 240 | 600 | 1200 |

*Hourly wages plus cost of office space, insurance, equipment, etc.

# How To Make Your Meetings More Effective

- Determine first of all, whether you really need to hold a meeting. Can you send a letter or memo instead? What about the telephone? What about a conference call?

- Plan your agenda in full detail before the meeting is called. List each item and send a notice at least a few days in advance so that everyone can prepare.

- As chairperson, you should anticipate different points of view likely to be raised for each agenda item and allow time accordingly, and be prepared to cut off discussion when time runs out.
  Generally, the one who writes the agenda has control of the meeting. Be sure that everyone sticks to it.

- Give the participants enough notice to attend the meeting. Remind them the day before and confirm their attendance. Give them every opportunity to state their opinion on agenda items before the meeting if they cannot attend.
  Avoid the situation where someone complains that they weren't consulted. Anticipate the need to check with so and so in order to keep peace.

- Be sure to start on time and end on time. Your time and that of your audience is the only non-renewable resource. Use it wisely!
  Be known as someone who sticks to the agenda and

no one will take advantage of you. They will look forward to dealing with you because you respect their time.

- Plan so that no one is allowed to waste participants' time. Let latecomers ask for an update at the end of the meeting. Discourage idle chit-chat.

- Discourage hecklers and anyone who disrupts the meeting. Show that you are fair but intolerant of anyone who abuses the opportunity to meet and deal with important business.

- Consider having a *fine* for lateness. Everyone should agree in advance how much the penalty should be and what the money collected will be used for – perhaps a charity or a coffee and donuts fund. Everyone will hate to be penalized for being late and you'll be able to start on time!

---

**Warning:**

**Re: Meetings, Speeches and Books. . .**

**Do not judge them by length. . .**

**I could have used twice as many words and shared only half as many tips. . .**

---

# How to Evaluate
# Your Presentation Skills

Each time your make a presentation you should rate yourself. Identify the elements that went well and the ones that could be improved. Do not worry about mistakes. Just think about how you will do it better next time.

## Evaluation Checklist

| Element | Good | Not Good | How to Improve |
|---|---|---|---|
| Opening | | | |
| Voice | | | |
| Delivery | | | |
| Content | | | |
| Gestures | | | |
| Eye-contact | | | |
| Posture | | | |
| Warm smile | | | |
| Use of visuals | | | |
| Handling of questions | | | |
| Closing | | | |
| Departure | | | |

# Three Questions
# to ask yourself
# After each Presentation

1. Was the purpose of my presentation clear to the audience and did I meet my declared objectives?

2. Did I keep within my scheduled time?

3. Did everyone receive a clear understanding of the action recommended in my closing message?

*Remember:*
*In presenting,*
*perception is reality*

*— Peter Urs Bender*

# The Process of Communicating

| 1. | Have a message worth communicating |  **NO** | Keep Quiet |

 **YES**

| 2. | Gain the listeners' attention, capture their interest, build their trust. |  **NO** | Get it! |

 **YES**

| 3. | Emphasize understanding |  **NO** | Say it Differently |

 **YES**

| 4. | Obtain Feedback |  **NO** | Emphasize Understanding |

 **YES**

| 5. | Watch your emotional tone |  **NO** | You Might Fail! |

 **YES**

| 6. | Persuade them and Close | **NO** | You Wasted Your Time! |

# Preparation – Presenting
# Pay Off

| | None | Lots |
|---|---|---|
| **Often** | O.K. But you could do much better! | Perfect! Now start finding new audiences and customize! |
| **Seldom** | You not only look silly ... you are! | You're in the right direction. Keep on going! |

**PRESENTING**

← **None**   **Lots** →

**P R E P A R A T I O N**

# More
# Secrets of Power Presenters

They:   Prepare a lot...
       Present a heck of a lot...
       Customize 10 – 20% for each audience...


And every time before a presentation
they go through the **Salt System**
    **S**eating
    **A**udio
    **L**ighting
    **T**emperature

*The great end of life
is not knowledge but
action.*

*— Thomas Henry Huxley*

## THE END!

You finally made it!
But, there is one more secret,
If you really want results,
go back and glance through this book
a few more times!

Positively,

N.B.   Referring to this book before each presentation will
ensure optimum results for both the speaker and
the audience.

To perfect, upgrade or maintain your presentation skills, I strongly suggest you join Toastmasters International.

You will find clubs throughout the country, in cities and most larger communities. A lot of corporations, military bases, churches, colleges and universities, as well as senior citizens, singles, and many other groups have their own clubs.

Interestingly, there are no individual instructors in any Toastmasters club. Members evaluate each others presentations and that is one reason their annual membership fee is so moderate.

The average club has 20 to 40 members. They meet once a week for about an hour and a half.

New members progress through a series of ten different speaking assignments. Each is designed to build the basic foundation of a good presentation.

The first Toastmasters club was established in California in 1924 by Dr. Ralph C. Smedley, a YMCA director. Today, Toastmasters International has helped more than 3 million people develop better communication and leadership skills. There are now over 8,000 chapters with more than 180,000 members in nearly 60 countries.

For more information check your phone book, call your Chamber of Commerce or contact the world office:

> Toastmasters International
> P.O. Box 9052
> Mission Viejo, CA 92690-7052
> Phone (714) 858-8255

If you are a more advanced speaker, a trainer or someone who would like to be a full time speaking professional, you must belong to N.S.A. and attend their winter workshops as well as their summer convention.

> National Speakers Association
> 1500 South Priest Dirve
> Tempe, Arizona 85281
> Phone (602) 968-2552

# Index

## QUOTATIONS & REFERENCES

Ash, Mary Kay, 62

Carnegie, Dale, 54, 114
Churchill, Winston, 56, 181
Confucius, 15, 32
Coolidge, Calvin, 28

Da Vinci, Leonardo, 107
Darwin, Charles, 105
De Gaulle, Charles, 191
Drucker, Peter F., 9, 37

Edison, Thomas, 29
Einstein, Albert, 51

Ford, Henry, 76, 186
Franklin, Benjamin, 100, 220

Goethe, Johan Wolfgang, 39

Hill, Napoleon, 42, 195
Huxley, Thomas Henry, 229

Johnson, Samuel, 49

Keller, Helen, 38

Leacock, Stephen B., 214
Lincoln, Abraham, 104, 184, 206
Lombardi, Vince, 118

Mehrabian, Albert, 103

Rossevelt, Theodore, 116

Shakespeare, William, 128
Shaw, George Bernard, 12, 53
Socrates, 102
Sophocles, 170
Syrus, Publilius, 202

Truman, Harry, 94

Unknown, 106, 113

# Peter Urs Bender, CSP

Peter left his native Switzerland in 1967 and arrived in Montreal on a bitterly cold February evening. He brought with him a few dollars, his accounting education and a lot of energy. He could not speak English and had never been an outstanding student. He had always been too shy to address a group.

In Toronto, Peter sold accounting system software and worked hard to develop his presentation skills. He joined the Toronto Speakers Club (similar to Toastmasters) in 1970 and later lectured at Ryerson University. During a twelve year period he taught courses in Business Management, Marketing for Bankers and Public Speaking.

Today, Mr. Bender is one of the country's top speakers, giving keynote speeches and seminars regularly to business people in growing companies across Canada, the United States, and Europe. He received his Certified Speaking Professional designation (CSP) in 1993 from the National Speakers Association.

The press calls him the **Business Presentation Guru** and his philosophy on presentation techniques has been quoted by the North American and European media. In 1995, he received the prestigious "Communication and Leadership" award from Toastmasters International.

He believes in both mental and physical fitness. When an older brother died from a heart attack at age 39, he lost 25 pounds, quit smoking and began to run every day. He has since completed 19 international marathons and in spite of his busy schedule, he still keeps physically active.

His motto is:

*If we do what we've always done, we'll
get what we've always gotten.*

For keynotes and seminars on "Power Presentations" or "Leadership From Within", contact Peter Urs Bender directly at (416) 491-6690.